THINKING LIKE A SAINT

FR. TIMOTHY M. GALLAGHER, O.M.V.

Thinking like a Saint

Discernment of Spirits in the Catholic Tradition

IGNATIUS PRESS SAN FRANCISCO

Cover design by Enrique J. Aguilar

ISBN 978-1-62164-656-3 (PB)
ISBN 978-1-64229-285-5 (eBook)
Library of Congress Control Number 2026931529
Printed in the United States of America ♾

CONTENTS

PREFACE

How do saints *think*? Normally, we picture them at prayer, gazing up at a shaft of light, or giving away their cloaks to the poor. But what happens when they meet the mess of everyday life? How do they make their daily decisions? When they are overrun by sadness, pain, boredom, or persecution, how do they keep their mind's eye fixed on hope and love? How do they listen to the voice of the Holy Spirit when they are walking down the street? When we read about their mystical visions, these can seem like dispatches from another world—a glimpse through the Hubble Space Telescope, a whirling galaxy far from our earth. We cannot help but wonder, "What do they have to do with us?" What would these holy men and women make of our workaday distractions: groceries, smartphones, Zoom calls, doctor appointments, and DMV lines? Saint Paul tells us that we have access to "the mind of Christ" (1 Cor 2:16), but how does that hold up when discouragement looms? Is it still possible to think like a saint?

Yes, it absolutely is. In fact, within the Church's rich tradition, there is a step-by-step guidebook to holy thinking: Saint Ignatius of Loyola's Rules for the Discernment of Spirits. For forty years, I have studied, written about, and taught Ignatius' fourteen rules.[1] I have presented them

[1] The rules "for the first week", as Ignatius titles them. Saint Ignatius of Loyola, *Spiritual Exercises*, no. 313 (hereafter cited as *SpirEx*). In this book, I do not discuss Ignatius' rules "for the second week" (*SpirEx* 329–36). For these, see Timothy Gallagher, O.M.V., *Spiritual Consolation: An Ignatian Guide for the*

in parishes and retreat houses; for laypeople, religious, seminarians, and priests; and for people of varying ethnic and educational backgrounds. This experience consistently confirms that, when these rules are presented in an accessible way, they possess unparalleled efficacy in helping listeners understand and overcome discouragement in the spiritual life—what Ignatius calls "spiritual desolation". Participants always say two things: "Why did no one ever tell us this before?" and "Everyone should know this." They are right.

Ignatius dedicates the majority of his fourteen rules precisely to helping us conquer discouragement and its associated temptations. With unequalled clarity and practicality, he supplies the necessary means for this. And while responding to such discouragement has been necessary at every time in history, it is especially urgent in our own time. Desolation is more widespread now than ever before. The causes are not far to seek, but the need for a remedy is pressing.

These rules originated in Saint Ignatius' own conversion at age thirty. Long months of convalescence from wounds in battle, combined with the (reluctant) reading of the lives of Jesus and the saints to pass the time, awakened an awareness of the stirrings in his heart relative to thoughts about living in different ways: one, a return to his earlier life of sin, and the other, an imitation of the saints whose lives he was reading. In perhaps the greatest understatement in his autobiography, he tells us that "una vez se le abrieron un poco los ojos" (one time, his eyes were

---

Greater Discernment of Spirits (Crossroad, 2007); *Ignatius of Loyola's Second Rules for Discernment: A User's Guide for Spiritual Directors* (Crossroad, 2023); *The More Discerning Priest: Mature Discernment in Priesthood* (Emmaus Road, 2026); "Second Week Rules for Greater Discernment", available at DiscerningHearts.com, on the Discerning Hearts app, and on YouTube.

opened a little).[2] That revelation changed his life forever, and with him, the lives of countless men and women to this day.

Continued reflection on his experience, an outpouring of God's grace, and the experience of many who quickly began to seek his help taught Ignatius that attention to the movements of the heart, with their related thoughts, reveals to us both God's leading in our lives and the lies of the enemy, the tempter. This awareness and understanding, he saw, frees us to pursue God's leading and to reject those lies. The fruit of such discernment is evident in his life of sanctity and in his service to the Church.

In the many years I have taught the discernment of spirits, I have witnessed such fruit in men and women who love the Lord. Discernment—that is, attention to the movements of our hearts and thoughts, an understanding of which are of God and which are of the enemy, and corresponding acceptance and rejection—*sets us free*, free from the burdens of the enemy and free to follow the Lord we love.

I have discussed Ignatius' fourteen rules in earlier books.[3] There, I explored these rules in themselves, unpacking the compact language Ignatius employs and illustrating the rules through examples. This book, because it covers the same rules, necessarily overlaps to some extent with my earlier books. But its purpose is different. Each chapter title provides a one-sentence summary of the rule as Ignatius teaches it, and each chapter consists of two parts: (1) a brief explanation

[2] "Autobiography", 8, in *San Ignacio de Loyola: Obras* (Biblioteca de Autores Cristianos, 2013), 31. I have discussed Ignatius' conversion experience in detail in the following: Timothy M. Gallagher, O.M.V., *The Discernment of Spirits: An Ignatian Guide to Everyday Living* (Crossroad, 2005), 11–15, and Timothy M. Gallagher, O.M.V., *Setting Captives Free: Personal Reflections on Ignatian Discernment of Spirits* (Crossroad, 2018), xx–xxvii.

[3] I list these in the section titled "Additional Resources" at the end of this book.

of the rule in question and (2) an extensive compilation of the work of other saints and spiritual figures who, in their own words, witness to the subtleties of that rule.

A fundamental truth underlies this approach. In the rules, Ignatius adds nothing to the spiritual life. He only (a life-changing "only") helps us to grasp the spiritual experience that always occurs in our hearts and thoughts. When people learn discernment, they *understand* their spiritual experience for the first time, and this is liberation, because now they can respond to it. On one occasion, after I had presented these rules, a woman said, "Before, I was reacting. Now, I'm responding"—a monumental transition. As we will see, Ignatius not only helps us notice and understand this experience but also supplies spiritual tools for responding to it.

In my four decades of teaching these rules, not one person has ever said to me, "I don't know what Ignatius is talking about." All of us do. In his rules, Ignatius describes universal experiences. It is no surprise, therefore, that we find similar teachings in other saints and spiritual writers: Saint Augustine, Saint Francis of Assisi, Saint Thomas Aquinas, Thomas à Kempis, Saint Teresa of Avila, Saint John of the Cross, Saint Francis de Sales, Jean-Pierre de Caussade, Saint Thérèse of Lisieux, Raïssa Maritain, and Servant of God Dorothy Day, to name only some. We will hear from these and many others in the following chapters. Most of those quoted are saints or people at various stages in the process of canonization. Others are lesser-known Catholic writers or speakers who have wisdom to share. There are also some classic authors who, though not Catholic, nevertheless offer sharp insights into certain spiritual realities—a confirmation of just how universal the rules are.

Clearly, then, Ignatius' principles are "Ignatian" only in their structure and wording. The experience described is that of *every* disciple of Jesus. Ignatius' gift, guided by the Spirit, was to perceive this experience clearly and express it succinctly, in an eminently practical way. His original text of the rules consists of 1,226 words—a little over three double-spaced typed pages. That Ignatius could condense such wisdom into so short a text is a marvelous feat of writing. At the same time, the text is quite complex, and its brevity calls for not only commentary but also testimony. Who better to witness to the rules' power than those who, like Ignatius, lived lives of holiness?

A book of this kind is necessary, as the best way—drawing on the wider Catholic spiritual tradition—of amplifying Ignatius' highly compact text.[4] Each chapter (after the introduction) focuses on one of the fourteen rules and consists of three sections: an exposition of the rule, brief personal reflections in its regard, and a wide selection of parallel quotes from the saints and spiritual writers mentioned. In this last section, I have italicized my comments to distinguish them from the text of the author cited.

In earlier books, I quoted a number of saints' experiences and writings. In this book, given its goal, I cite many more. With few exceptions, the quotations given are new with respect to the earlier writing. For those who wish a complete picture of these quotations—those in the earlier books as well as those offered here—I list the quotations cited in my earlier books in a final footnote to each chapter.

It is a delight, as I continue to read and as people share their experiences, to see ever further reflections of the rules

[4] Darío López Tejada, S.J., does something of this kind in his *Los ejercicios espirituales de San Ignacio de Loyola: Comentario y textos afines* (Edibesa, 1998). Because he comments on the entirety of the Spiritual Exercises, his selection of texts is necessarily limited with respect to the present book, which is focused only on the First Week Rules for discernment. I have included two quotes from Tejada in chapters 7 and 11. In each case, citations are included in footnotes.

for discernment of spirits. The experiences and quotations I present here are found either in published works, for which I give the reference, or in personal experiences, always shared with permission. When no reference is given, the thoughts and experiences are my own.

A double benefit emerges from the pairing of Ignatius' rules with the wisdom of other saints. On the one hand, the compressed wording of the rules is enhanced and enfleshed by rich sources in our Catholic spiritual tradition; on the other, our consciousness of their rootedness in that tradition is solidified. May reading this book bring clarity and encouragement on your spiritual journey.

TEXT OF SAINT IGNATIUS' RULES FOR DISCERNMENT

Rules for becoming aware and understanding to some extent the different movements that are caused in the soul, the good, to receive them, and the bad to reject them. And these rules are more proper for the first week.

First Rule. In persons who are going from mortal sin to mortal sin, the enemy is ordinarily accustomed to propose apparent pleasures to them, leading them to imagine sensual delights and pleasures in order to hold them more and make them grow in their vices and sins. In these persons the good spirit uses a contrary method, stinging and biting their consciences through their rational power of moral judgment.

Second Rule. In persons who are going on intensely purifying their sins and rising from good to better in the service of God our Lord, the method is contrary to that in the first rule. For then it is proper to the evil spirit to bite, sadden, and place obstacles, disquieting with false reasons, so that the person may not go forward. And it is proper to the good spirit to give courage and strength, consolations, tears, inspirations and quiet, easing and taking away all obstacles, so that the person may go forward in doing good.

SpirEx 313–27. All quotations from this source are the author's translation. See Timothy Gallagher, O.M.V., *The Discernment of Spirits: An Ignatian Guide to Everyday Living* (Crossroad, 2005), 7–10 (with slight modifications in accordance with the original manuscript and with a different metaphor in rule 12). See the following note on page 16.

Third Rule. The third is of spiritual consolation. I call it consolation when some interior movement is caused in the soul, through which the soul comes to be inflamed with love of its Creator and Lord, and, consequently when it can love no created thing on the face of the earth in itself, but only in the Creator of them all. Likewise, when it sheds tears that move to love of its Lord, whether out of sorrow for one's sins, or for the passion of Christ our Lord, or because of other things directly ordered to his service and praise. Finally, I call consolation every increase of hope, faith, and charity, and all interior joy that calls and attracts to heavenly things and to the salvation of one's soul, quieting it and giving it peace in its Creator and Lord.

Fourth Rule. The fourth is of spiritual desolation. I call desolation all the contrary of the third rule, such as darkness of soul, disturbance in it, movement to low and earthly things, disquiet from various agitations and temptations, moving to lack of confidence, without hope, without love, finding oneself totally slothful, tepid, sad, and as if separated from one's Creator and Lord. For just as consolation is contrary to desolation, in the same way the thoughts that come from consolation are contrary to the thoughts that come from desolation.

Fifth Rule. In time of desolation never make a change, but be firm and constant in the proposals and determination in which one was the day preceding such desolation, or in the determination in which one was in the preceding consolation. Because, as in consolation the good spirit guides and counsels us more, so in desolation the bad spirit, with whose counsels we cannot find the way to a right decision.

Sixth Rule. Although in desolation we should not change our first proposals, it is very advantageous to change ourselves intensely against the desolation itself, as by insisting more upon prayer, meditation, upon much examination, and upon extending ourselves in some suitable way of doing penance.

Seventh Rule. Let one who is in desolation consider how the Lord has left him in trial in his natural powers, so that he may resist the various agitations and temptations of the enemy; because he can resist with the divine help, which always remains with him, though he does not clearly feel it; for the Lord has taken away from him his great fervor, abundant love, and intense grace, leaving him, however, sufficient grace for eternal salvation.

Eighth Rule. Let one who is in desolation work to be in patience, which is contrary to the vexations that come to him, and let him think that he will soon be consoled, diligently using the means against such desolation, as is said in the sixth rule.

Ninth Rule. There are three principal causes for which we find ourselves desolate. The first is because we are tepid, slothful, or negligent in our spiritual exercises, and so through our faults spiritual consolation withdraws from us. The second, to try us and see how much we are and how much we extend ourselves in his service and praise without so much payment of consolations and increased graces. The third, to give us true recognition and understanding so that we may interiorly feel that it is not ours to attain or maintain increased devotion, intense love, tears, or any other spiritual consolation, but that all is the gift and grace of God our Lord, and so that we may not build a nest in something belonging to another, raising our mind in some pride or vainglory, attributing to ourselves the devotion or the other parts of the spiritual consolation.

Tenth Rule. Let one who is in consolation think how he will conduct himself in the desolation that will come after, taking new strength for that time.

Eleventh Rule. Let one who is consoled seek to humble himself and lower himself as much as he can, thinking of how little he is capable in the time of desolation without such grace or consolation. On the contrary, let one who is in desolation think that he can do much with God's sufficient grace to resist all his enemies, taking strength in his Creator and Lord.

Twelfth Rule. The enemy acts as spoiled children do in being weak when faced with strength and strong when faced with weakness. For it is proper to spoiled children, when they begin to act out, to lose heart and desist when their parents confront them firmly; and, on the contrary, if their parents respond with weakness and helplessness, their acting out grows greatly and knows no bounds.[1] In the same way, it is proper to the enemy to weaken and lose heart, fleeing and ceasing his temptations when the person who is exercising himself in spiritual things confronts the temptations of the enemy firmly, doing what is diametrically opposed to them; and, on the contrary, if the person who is exercising himself begins to be afraid and lose heart in suffering the temptations, there is no beast so fierce on the face of the earth as the enemy of human nature in following out his damnable intention with such growing malice.

Thirteenth Rule. Likewise, he conducts himself as a false lover in wishing to remain secret and not be revealed. For a dissolute man who, speaking with evil intention, makes dishonorable advances to a daughter of a good father or a wife of a good husband, wishes his words and

[1] I have changed Ignatius' metaphor here (that of a woman fighting with a man) to avoid distraction from the point he wishes to illustrate. David Fleming, S.J., also adopts the metaphor of the spoiled child in *Draw Me into Your Friendship: A Literal Translation and a Contemporary Reading of the Spiritual Exercises* (Institute of Jesuit Sources, 1996), 257.

persuasions to be secret, and the contrary displeases him very much, when the daughter reveals to her father or the wife to her husband his false words and depraved intention, because he easily perceives that he will not be able to succeed with the undertaking begun. In the same way, when the enemy of human nature brings his wiles and persuasions to the just soul, he wishes and desires that they be received and kept in secret; but when one reveals them to one's good confessor or to another spiritual person, who knows his deceits and malicious designs, it weighs on him very much, because he perceives that he will not be able to succeed with the malicious undertaking he has begun, because his manifest deceits have been revealed.

Fourteenth Rule. Likewise, he conducts himself as a leader, intent upon conquering and robbing what he desires. For, just as a captain and leader of an army in the field, pitching his camp and exploring the fortifications and defenses of a stronghold, attacks it at the weakest point, in the same way the enemy of human nature, roving about, looks in turn at all our theological, cardinal, and moral virtues; and where he finds us weakest and most in need for our eternal salvation, there he attacks us and attempts to take us.

INTRODUCTION

Awareness, Understanding, Action

On the Title Statement of the Rules for Discernment

Saint Ignatius of Loyola introduces his rules with a brief and densely packed title statement:

> Rules for becoming aware and understanding to some extent the different movements that are caused in the soul, the good, to receive them, and the bad to reject them.[1]

These are, he tells us, *rules*: practical guidelines. They are short, essential statements that clarify spiritual experience and supply tools for responding to it. Ignatius provides us with fourteen such rules.

[1] *SpirEx* 313. Because the fourteen rules follow immediately upon para. 313 in the *Spiritual Exercises*, I will not supply the subsequent paragraph numbers when citing the text of the individual rules. Para. 313 contains a further sentence, "And these rules are more proper for the first week", which situates them within Ignatius' thirty-day retreat. "Ignatius informs us of the setting in which these rules are most likely to operate: the 'first week' of the Spiritual Exercises, that is, the stage of the spiritual journey in which we seek growing freedom from sinfulness and greater readiness to love and serve God—the state in which many of us are likely to find ourselves." Timothy M. Gallagher, O.M.V., *Setting Captives Free: Personal Reflections on Ignatian Discernment of Spirits* (Crossroad, 2018), xxvii.

Three Steps in Discernment

Ignatius articulates this response to spiritual experience according to three consecutive steps: (1) Be *aware* of the experience; (2) work with the tools Ignatius supplies to *understand* what is of God and what is not of God in this experience; and (3) *take action* accordingly, by *accepting* what is of God and *rejecting* what is not.

The focus of these three steps is "the different *movements* that are caused in the soul"—that is, the stirrings of our hearts (affective experience) and the thoughts (cognitive experience) that accompany them. A man, for example, is disheartened after a difficult day at work (affective experience) and considers omitting his habitual prayer before retiring (cognitive experience). A woman feels God's closeness and love after a fruitful time of prayer (affective experience) and considers new steps in her spiritual life (cognitive experience).

In regard to this daily spiritual experience, Ignatius calls us to be aware, understand, and take action, accepting or rejecting. The following paradigm emerges:

1. Be aware.
2. Understand.
3. Take action: Accept or reject.

In the fourteen rules that follow, Ignatius will show us how to do this.

Three Actors in Discernment

Adhering to Ignatius' own vocabulary, we will call these actors the *person* discerning, the *good spirit*, and the *enemy*.

Each of us, as he experiences these movements of the heart and their related thoughts, is the *person* discerning.

The *good spirit* is, above all, God, the Holy Spirit, who works in the hearts of his sons and daughters whom he loves. *Good spirit* also signifies the work of God's angels on our behalf; the supernatural organism implanted in us through Baptism: the indwelling of the Trinity, sanctifying grace, the virtues, the gifts of the Holy Spirit, and personal charisms; and good influences around us—that is to say, *good spirit* denotes God and all those influences that are from God and directed toward God.

The *enemy* is Satan and his associated fallen angels, assisted by the wound of concupiscence we bear from original sin and the harmful influences in the world around us.[2] Ignatius' often-repeated word *enemy* is well chosen: This is the one who is inimical to, against, what God intends for the human person.

Simply to know that all three actors are real and operative in the spiritual life is enormously clarifying.[3]

A key observation regarding the good spirit and the enemy follows from what we have said: While both actors are real and are operative in our spiritual lives and it is important to be aware of both, they are not equal. The enemy is, yes, of a higher order than we, but he is still no more than a fallen creature. The good spirit is the infinite, eternal, omnipotent, loving, and personally close God. Discernment, as Ignatius envisions it, is a spirituality of grace, of redemption, of hope.

[2] This is the classic triad, "the world, the flesh, and the devil". See, for example, John of the Cross, *The Dark Night*, in *The Collected Works of St. John of the Cross*, 3rd ed., trans. Kieran Kavanaugh, O.C.D., and Otilio Rodriguez, O.C.D. (ICS Publications, 1991), 391.

[3] "I presuppose that there are three thoughts in me, that is, one that is my own, which arises entirely from my own freedom and desire; and two others that come from without, one that comes from the good spirit and the other from the bad spirit." *SpirEx* 32.

Three Levels of Human Experience

The human person is a unity, but human experience includes three different levels: (1) the *physical*, (2) the *psychological*, and (3) the *spiritual*. In his rules, Ignatius focuses on the spiritual level—the level of grace, of faith, of our relationship with God. This does not signify, however, that the physical and psychological levels have no significance for the spiritual level. They very much do.

A classic principle expresses, "Gratia praesupponit perficitque naturam" (Grace presupposes nature and perfects it). God's grace in us—our spiritual life—presupposes what occurs on our physical and psychological levels and elevates it. Grace presupposes human nature, our bodily and emotional humanity. Consequently, what happens on these two levels significantly affects what happens on the level of grace. We will see this truth at work as we explore Ignatius' fourteen rules.

Our effort to do this rests upon a specifically Christian anthropology—that is, the human person understood in the light of Christ. The psychiatrist Karl Stern writes that when the human person is so understood, "the whole of anthropology as conceived by philosophers and psychologists is at once deepened in a very peculiar way. It is as if a great, but albeit two-dimensional, picture received a third dimension and came to life."[4] When all three dimensions of the human person are recognized and when all three work together, wonderful growth follows. Ignatius' rules take this Christian anthropology seriously and offer a practical way of interpreting (discerning) what in our hearts and thoughts is of God and what is of the enemy, providing tools for accepting the first and rejecting the second.

[4] Karl Stern, *The Pillar of Fire* (Harcourt, Brace, 1951), 228.

A Note on Awareness

Awareness of our hearts and thoughts is the indispensable portal to discernment. Without this awareness, the subsequent steps of understanding and action are not possible. Thus, we should not pass quickly by Ignatius' reference to it.

Reviewing his years far from God, Saint Augustine writes, "Intus eras, et ego foris" (You were within, and I was without).[5] *Within*: in touch with, conscious of, aware of God's action in our hearts and thoughts. *Without*: occupied with endless activity, immersed in concerns, plans, projects ... and unaware of God's action within. For Ignatius, the transition from without to within occurred when, on his convalescent bed, "his eyes were opened a little" and he first noticed the spiritual experience that occurred in his heart and thoughts. This awareness transformed his life. It can do so for us as well. The discerning life calls us to this blessed transition.

We cannot take such awareness for granted. Much militates against it: the need for an understanding of spiritual experience and for a vocabulary to express it; a secular culture that does not recognize spiritual experience; the effort required to be within in the face of an easier, more immediate focus without; the difficulty in focusing within in the dispersion of the digital age; the multiplicity and rapid shifts of our emotions and thoughts; human sinfulness; discouraging tactics of the enemy; the pressure of a culture that imposes busyness as a way of life; and other like factors.[6]

I believe that the tendency to live without derives most deeply from the flight from our limitations that Blaise Pascal

[5] *Confessions* 10, 27, author's translation.

[6] On what hinders and helps this awareness, see Gallagher, *Setting Captives Free*, xxix–xxxiii, and Timothy Gallagher, O.M.V., *The Discernment of Spirits: An Ignatian Guide to Everyday Living* (Crossroad, 2005), 17–20.

calls *diversion*.[7] Because it is troubling to face our mortality and our spiritual, moral, and emotional limitations, it seems easier, even if unsatisfying, to *divert* our awareness without.

This changes when the human heart learns that to be within, far more than to face human limitation, is to encounter the eternal, warm, infinite, personally close, and loving presence of the Savior. Then the heart is no longer afraid. Thus, evangelization (learning that there is a Savior, the Lord Jesus), catechesis (growing in knowledge of this faith), and discipleship (the sacraments, prayer, life in the Church) always precede discernment.

Because grace presupposes nature, when we deepen our natural contemplative capacity, we also increase our spiritual capacity to be within: gazing at the beauties of nature, sitting peacefully before a fire, listening to beautiful music, reading, quietly studying, paying attention to the people around us—all of these foster increased access to the discerning life on the spiritual level. The philosopher Martin Buber quotes a rabbi as saying, "A human being who has not a single hour for his own every day is no human being."[8]

The Rules Today

When I began teaching the rules for discernment in the 1980s, I found a certain resistance to the idea of rules. Rules are confining. They limit freedom. Our culture has always disliked rules: "Don't tread on me." "Live free or die." "Just do it." Some of this opposition to rules remains today, but in the forty-plus years since then, I have seen a notable

[7] *Pensées*, 139.

[8] Martin Buber, *Tales of the Hasidim: The Later Masters* (Schocken Books, 1948), 92.

change. When a culture leaves its members adrift, confused, and uncertain of how to proceed in life, then short, effective guidelines become attractive. They provide clear paths toward our goals. Today, rules are everywhere: in bestselling books (a search for "rules" in Amazon books brings up over 60,000 titles), on the web, in music, and elsewhere. Five hundred years ago, Saint Ignatius composed a set of fourteen clear, practical, and effective rules for becoming aware of, understanding, and responding to the often-confusing spiritual experience in our hearts and thoughts.

I mentioned earlier that Christian anthropology is the one integral understanding of the human person. According to the Vatican II constitution *Gaudium et Spes*, "The truth is that only in the mystery of the incarnate Word does the mystery of man take on light."[9] This means that to understand the human person fully, one must include the supernatural dimension of our humanity: the role of God, of Jesus our Savior, of grace, of the supernatural virtues, of the gifts of the Holy Spirit, of the enemy, of his lies, of his temptations, and the rest. Saint Ignatius' rules for discernment take this Christian anthropology seriously and offer a practical way of interpreting (discerning) what in our hearts and thoughts is of God and what is of the enemy. His rules then provide tools for accepting the first and rejecting the second. This is no small contribution to current efforts to foster healing and growth.

Ignatius changed when he became aware of heart-level stirrings relative to thoughts of living in two different ways: the one sinful, the other holy. He noticed that the first set of thoughts left him sad, the second, happy. When he

[9] Vatican Council II, Pastoral Constitution on the Church in the Modern World *Gaudium et Spes* (December 7, 1965), no. 22, https://www.vatican.va/archive/hist_councils/ii_vatican_council/documents/vat-ii_const_19651207_Gaudium-et-spes_en.html.

understood that the second was of God, he took action to pursue it—and a path to sanctity began, with great blessing for the Church. This is why it is so important that we, too, know these rules and live with this awareness.

Ignatius' teaching on discernment of spirits was born in the moment that his eyes were "opened a little". Who can say what God will do in your life if your spiritual eyes, too, are opened a little?

We need, therefore, to habituate ourselves to times of quiet and silence, to a slower pace, to openness to the richness of life around us. One simple and not insignificant application: If we have not set at least one limit on the use of our phones, we are spending too much time on them. The more this is the case, the less spiritually aware we will be.

Once, however, we slow down enough to hear what is happening within us, we can begin discerning the spirits at work. Mary is our model—she who "kept all these things, reflecting on them in her heart" (Lk 2:19, NABRE). Mary, the Mother of Good Counsel, the Virgin Most Prudent, the Seat of Wisdom guides us with maternal tenderness toward a discerning heart.

Witnesses to Awareness, Understanding, and Action

Saint Augustine

Return to your heart: why go from yourselves, and perish from yourselves? Why go the ways of solitude? You go astray by wandering: return. Where? To the Lord. 'Tis quickly done: first return to your own heart; you have wandered abroad an exile from yourself; you know not yourself, and yet you are asking by whom you were made!

Return, return to your heart, lift yourself away from the body.... Return to your heart; see there what, it may be, you can perceive of God, for in it is the image of God. In the inner man dwells Christ, in the inner man are you renewed after the image of God.[10]

Saint Thomas Aquinas

On the enemy's attempts to harm us, the good spirit's action on our behalf, and why God permits the first and gives the second:

Two things may be considered in the assault of the demons—the assault itself [*impugnatio*], and the ordering thereof [*ordo impugnationis*]. The assault itself is due to the malice of the demons, who through envy endeavor to hinder man's progress; and through pride usurp a semblance of divine power, by deputing certain ministers to assail man, as the angels of God in their various offices minister to man's salvation. But the ordering of the assault is from God, who knows how to make orderly use of evil by ordering it to good. On the other hand, in regard to the angels, both their guardianship [*custodia*] and the ordering thereof [*ordo custodiae*] are to be referred to God as their first author.[11]

[10] Augustine, *Tractates (Lectures) on the Gospel of John*, tractate 18, para. 10, https://www.newadvent.org/fathers/1701018.htm.

[11] *Summa Theologica*, trans. Fathers of the English Dominican Province, vol. 1 (Christian Classics, 1981), I, q. 114, a. 1, co., p. 556. On the harmony between Ignatian discernment of God's will and Thomistic prudence, see David M. Gallagher and Timothy M. Gallagher, O.M.V., "Ignatian Discernment and Thomistic Prudence: Opposition or Harmony?" *The Way* 60, no. 2 (2021): 18–36, https://www.theway.org.uk/websubs/602.pdf. See also the Cardinal Stafford Lecture on the same topic by the same authors at https://sjvdenver.edu/lectures/.

The enemy and good spirit are real, and they act for opposite ends. The assault of the enemy is from malice and pride; the permitting of this lies within God's providence (his ordering): if, with his grace, we respond well, we grow in the spiritual life. Ignatius addresses this in rules 7 and 9.

Cardinal Robert Sarah

Great things begin in the desert, in silence, in poverty, in abandonment. Look at Moses, Elijah, John the Baptist, and Jesus himself.[12]

All that is from God makes no noise. Nothing is sudden, everything is delicate, pure, and silent.[13]

Adoration of the Blessed Sacrament is a time when the quality of interior silence can allow us to enter a little into God's silence.[14]

Søren Kierkegaard

Oh, if one might (as surely one is justified in doing from a Christian point of view), if, in view of the present situation of the world, of life as a whole, one might Christianly say, "It is a sickness"—and if I were a physician, and someone asked me, "What do you think must be done?", I should answer, "The first, the unconditional condition of

[12] *The Power of Silence: Against the Dictatorship of Noise* (Ignatius Press, 2017), no. 104, 64.

[13] *The Power of Silence*, no. 365, 187.

[14] *The Power of Silence*, no. 192, 99.

doing anything, and therefore the first thing to be done is, procure silence, introduce silence, God's Word cannot be heard, and if, served by noisy expedients, it is to be shouted out clamorously so as to be heard in the midst of the din, it is no longer God's Word. Procure silence! Everything contributes to the noise; and as it is said of a hot drink that it stirs the blood, so in our times, every event, even the most insignificant, every communication, even the most fatuous, is calculated merely to harrow the senses or to stir up the masses, the crowd, the public, to make a noise. And man, the shrewd [mind], has become sleepless in the effort to find out new, ever new means for increasing the noise, for spreading abroad, with the greatest possible speed, and on the greatest possible scale, the meaningless racket. Indeed, the apogee has almost been attained: communication has just about reached the lowest point, with respect to its importance; and contemporaneously the means of communication have pretty nearly attained the highest point, with respect to quick and overwhelming distribution. For what is in such haste to get out, and on the other hand what has such widespread distribution as ... [drivel]? Oh, procure silence!"[15]

Yes, procure silence; create silence. Only with times of silence can the "still small voice" (1 Kings 19:12) be heard; only in this way is awareness possible.

[15] *For Self-Examination and Judge for Yourselves! and Three Discourses, 1851*, trans. Walter Lowrie (Oxford University Press, 1946), 71–72. The editor, commenting in 1946, adds, "It is to be remembered that the means of communication S. K. was thinking of were only the newspaper (his special abhorrence) and the telegraph (which was just coming into use)—and yet from this passage one might suppose that he had in view the telephone, wireless telegraphy, the radio, the news reel, not to speak of other modern means of making a noise", 72n1. I have changed "pate" to "mind" and "twaddle" to "drivel".

Saint John of the Cross

What we need most in order to make progress is to be silent before this great God with our appetite and with our tongue, for the language he best hears is silent love.[16]

Simone Weil

Something in our soul has a far more violent repugnance for true attention than the flesh has for bodily fatigue. This something is much more closely connected with evil than is the flesh. That is why every time that we really concentrate our attention, we destroy the evil in ourselves. If we concentrate with this intention, a quarter of an hour of attention is better than a great many good works.[17]

Julien Green (Novelist)

Yesterday evening, in the chapel of Foreign Missions, rue du Bac. There were present a very old white-bearded priest, four nuns in black, and two or three laymen, all absorbed in such deep meditation that for twenty minutes I did not hear the least sound, and had I closed my eyes, I might have believed myself completely alone. There was something magnificent in this silence. Father

[16] *The Sayings of Light and Love*, in *The Collected Works of St. John of the Cross*, 3rd ed., trans. Kieran Kavanaugh, O.C.D., and Otilio Rodriguez, O.C.D. (ICS Publications, 1991), 95.

[17] "Reflections on the Right Use of School Studies with a View to the Love of God", https://www.themathesontrust.org/papers/christianity/Weil-Reflections.pdf.

Surin says that God visits souls only when they are *still and empty.*[18]

Jean-Pierre de Caussade, S.J.

There is never a moment when God does not come forward in the guise of some suffering or some duty, and all that takes place within us, around us and through us both includes and hides his activity. Yet, because it is invisible, we are always taken by surprise and do not recognize his operation until it has passed by us. If we could lift the veil and if we watched with vigilant attention, God would endlessly reveal himself to us and we should see and rejoice in his active presence in all that befalls us. At every event we should exclaim: "It is the Lord!" (John 21:7).[19]

Is Father de Caussade right? Does God's activity in our lives always take us by surprise? Do we see it only when it has passed us by? What if we lived with discerning awareness? What if we were aware of God's activity in the moment? What if we could, to use Ignatius' classic phrase, "find God in all things"?

David Morrison (Catholic Writer)

I have brought silence back into my life. Each day I let myself have about an hour of radio in the morning [written twenty-five years ago: today, limit the use of digital devices], enough to hear the news headlines and pick up

[18] *Diary, 1928–1957*, ed. Kurt Wolff, trans. Anne Green (Harcourt, Brace & World, 1964), 297.

[19] *Abandonment to Divine Providence*, trans. John Beevers (Image Books, 1975), 36.

a weather forecast. But then I turn it off and let the audio space around me empty until the only steady sounds are the throbbing burst as the furnace kicks on or the low whir of the computer. I love how, in the silence, my mind turns so quickly to prayer. Fragments of conversations from yesterday or topics I had marked in my mind to raise to God come bubbling out in prayers as I work. Snatches of favorite hymns come to mind to hum, and I find that although the day moves as quickly as it ever did, I generally feel less stressed at the end of it.[20]

Raïssa Maritain

Self-examination every day, at a set hour.... Be attentive to divine impressions. Be attentive to all the movements of my heart.[21]

From *The Sayings of Holy Abba Poemen*

Abba Poemen said, "Vigilance, self-knowledge and discernment; these are the guides of the soul."[22]

[20] *New Covenant*, May 2000, 17.

[21] *Raïssa's Journal*, ed. Jacques Maritain (Magi, 1974), 103.

[22] Saying no. 35, https://www.johnsanidopoulos.com/2016/08/the-life-and-sayings-of-holy-abba_27.html. For complementary quotations, see Gallagher, *The Discernment of Spirits*: St. Ignatius (11–15), St. Augustine (17–18), John Cassian (18–19), Blaise Pascal (19–20); Gallagher, *Setting Captives Free*: St. Ignatius (xx–xxvii), St. John Henry Newman (xxx), Simone Weil (xxx), Thomas Merton (xxx), Blaise Pascal (xxxii).

Rule 1

If You Are Running Away, Turn Around

Ignatius begins with discernment in the person who is far from God. His first rule reads:

> First Rule. In persons who are going from mortal sin to mortal sin, the enemy is ordinarily accustomed to propose apparent pleasures to them, leading them to imagine sensual delights and pleasures in order to hold them more and make them grow in their vices and sins. In these persons the good spirit uses a contrary method, stinging and biting their consciences through their rational power of moral judgment.

In this rule, Ignatius addresses "persons who are going from mortal sin to mortal sin"—that is, persons who are far from God and living in confirmed serious sin. Both the enemy and the good spirit work in such persons, whether to facilitate this way of life (the enemy) or to hinder it (the good spirit).

Before their respective conversions, both Saint Augustine and Saint Ignatius exemplify this spiritual state. Consider what this often looks like in today's culture: A college sophomore stopped going to church when he left home two years ago. He engages in loose living and all that attends this: irresponsibility, shallow relationships, misuse of sex, and abuse of substances. A married businessman has not been to church for twenty years, is not always faithful to his wife, and is willing to engage in seriously dishonest business practices when it serves his end. In these and similar situations, rule 1 applies.

When people live in this unhappy state, Ignatius says, "the enemy is *ordinarily accustomed* to propose apparent pleasures to them." In these rules, Ignatius describes the ways that both the good and the bad spirits will ordinarily act. Knowing this, we more readily attain the understanding that permits appropriate action (accept or reject).

In such persons, Ignatius says, the enemy fills the imagination with images of sensual pleasures, "in order to hold them more and make them grow in their vices and sins". To the extent that they dwell on such images, they will be drawn to pursue this way of life.[1]

The enemy's use of the imagination is the more significant today in our "culture of the image". The college sophomore puts down the phone at 11:30 P.M. after an hour and a half of scrolling on social media. What kind of images fill his imagination? Which spirit is at work? The married businessman clicks off the remote at 1:00 A.M. after two hours of channel surfing. What kind of images fill his imagination? Which spirit is at work?

But grace is always the final word for Ignatius. The good spirit, he writes, "uses a contrary method". A law of contrariety holds throughout the experience Ignatius envisages in

[1] Michael Ivens, S.J., comments on "sensual delights and pleasures" as follows: "By *sensual delights* one is to understand not only (or even primarily) crass hedonism, but the gratification of any instinct—e.g. for power, wealth, fame—insofar as the instinct is not integrated into, and ordered by, a true relationship to Christ." *Understanding the Spiritual Exercises: Text and Commentary; A Handbook for Retreat Directors* (Gracewing, Inigo, 1998), 212–13. On this point, see Timothy M. Gallagher, O.M.V., *Setting Captives Free: Personal Reflections on Ignatian Discernment of Spirits* (Crossroad, 2018),12.

these fourteen rules: If the enemy does one thing, the good spirit will do exactly the contrary, and vice versa. The contrary quality of the two spirits' actions grows increasingly apparent as we begin to apply these rules and is a great help in reaching the understanding that permits action.

The work of the good spirit in people who are living in mortal sin is troubling to them. The good spirit stings these persons' consciences through "their rational power of moral judgment". In these persons, the enemy works in the imagination while the good spirit works in the conscience. The good spirit inspires troubling thoughts and disturbing questions that reveal to these persons the unhappiness of their situation and prompt them to the one change that can make them happy: to turn away from sin and turn toward the God who loves them and even now lovingly calls them back.

Consider the married businessman and his wife who had a long, ugly, intense fight over a trivial domestic matter last night. Both knew the problem was not that matter but the terrible damage he has done to their marriage and family.

Today, he is driving home from work. In God's providence, the radio is off and the phone is silenced. Light traffic on the highway leaves him free to recall that unhappy conflict the evening before. He sees again the pain in his wife's face, the suffering in her eyes; he hears again the bitterness of her words. He knows she is right. Thoughts arise in the silence: "Why have you done such severe harm to your marriage? Why have you caused your wife such intense pain? When your children are old enough to know how you are living, what will they think of you? What will happen to your relationship with them? Are you proud of yourself when you cheat a client who trusts you?"

These questions sting, bite, and trouble the man. This is the action of the good spirit, God's loving assault on his heart, calling him to the only change that can make him happy. If he is open to this action of the good spirit—if he accepts it—he will make that change. He says to himself, "I can't go on like this. Something has to change." He decides to call his pastor, and they meet. The meeting includes the Sacrament of Reconciliation, and a new life begins.

In that moment, this man is also free, if he chooses, to *reject* this action of the good spirit. He turns on the radio or activates his phone. He distracts himself from the stinging and biting that can change his life, and the opportunity is lost. We can be totally confident, however, that God will not give up on him. He will knock again.

Rule 1 tells us that God *never stops* working in the human heart, that he loves his sons and daughters too much ever simply to let them go, that he is willing to sting and bite in their hearts, ever calling them back to the one source of their joy in this life and in eternity.

The Sweetness of the Sting

Once, a woman was teaching this rule to a group in her parish. Many parents and grandparents were present. When she spoke of the stinging and biting of the good spirit in those far from God, a sense of lightness entered the room. To know that God never stops working in their children and grandchildren who are not practicing the faith gave new hope to the participants.

Imagine that a person living in serious sin comes to you and shares the bitterness, the burden, the distress he feels. For him, his pain is the sign of how far God has withdrawn from him. When, with Ignatius, you show him that, on the contrary, this trouble of heart is the surest sign that God has always loved him too much to let him go, it melts something in his heart.

If you have ever experienced the unhappy spiritual situation described in rule 1, you look back with deep gratitude to God for the "stinging and biting", the heaviness of heart, the unhappiness, the sense of emptiness that led you to the change that brought peace and joy to your life.

A Note on Images

Two blocks from where I live is a small burger bar, with booths on either side of a short aisle. Ten large television screens display an endless succession of images. Today, images are everywhere: on our televisions, computers, mobile devices, phones, and watches; in stores; on billboards. Images can do great good, such as when people watch an inspiring movie, contemplate a lovely painting, or view a beautiful church. But images can also do great harm and serve the tactic of the enemy just described. For this reason, we must strive to fill our lives with uplifting and noble images and avoid harmful ones. The enemy cannot use the images we never see.

Witnesses to Rule 1

Saint Thomas Aquinas

On how the evil one induces a person to sin:

Now the intellect, of its very nature, is moved by that which enlightens it in the knowledge of truth, which the devil has no intention of doing in man's regard; rather does he darken man's reason so that it may consent to sin, which darkness is due to the imagination and sensitive appetite. Consequently the operation of the devil seems to be confined to the imagination and sensitive appetite, by moving either of which he can induce man to sin. For his operation may result in presenting certain forms to the imagination; and he is able to incite the sensitive appetite to some passion or other.[2]

Patrick Madrid (Catholic Author and Speaker)

Of the year leading to his conversion:

In time, the effects of my years of immoderation and lukewarmness began to catch up with me. I can't recall when the feeling started but I eventually became aware of a growing sense of discontent and restlessness.... I was empty inside, a vacuum of selfishness where my interior life with Christ should have been. I grew frustrated about who I was and wanted to know what I was supposed to do with my life.... I grew deeply troubled about my past and present sinfulness.... Over the course of that year, my conscience prodded me ruthlessly. By now ... I was working in sales. I enjoyed my new work and was successful at it, but even that didn't muffle the anxiety and discontent that rang like a bell in the gathering dark night of my soul.[3]

Hutchins Hapgood (Author)

Narrating "Jim's" story of his life of crime:

On one of my trips to the City of Brotherly Love I had a poetical experience. The graft [stealing] had been good,

[2] *Summa Theologica*, trans. Fathers of the English Dominican Province, vol. 2 (Christian Classics, 1981), I-II, q. 80, a. 2, co., p. 949.

[3] "Confessions of a Guilty Bystander", in *Surprised by Truth 2: Fifteen Men and Women Give the Biblical and Historical Reasons for Becoming Catholic*, ed. Patrick Madrid (Sophia Institute Press, 2000), 174–76.

and one Sunday morning I left Dan and Patsy asleep, and went for a walk in the country, intending, for a change, to observe the day of rest. I walked for several hours through a beautiful, quiet country, and about ten o'clock passed a country church. They were singing inside, and for some reason, probably because I had had a good walk in the country, the music affected me strangely. I entered, and saw a blind evangelist and his sister. I bowed my head, and my whole past life came over me. Although everything had been coming my way, I felt uneasy, and thought of home for the first time in many weeks. I went back to the hotel in Philadelphia, feeling very gloomy, and shut myself up in my room.[4]

Charles Péguy

Commenting on the parable of the prodigal son:

> It has awakened in the heart a certain point of resonance
> A special resonance.
> It has also been especially fortunate.
> It is famous even among the impious.
> It has found, even with them, a point of entry.
> Alone perhaps it has remained driven into the heart of
> the impious
> Like a nail of tenderness.[5]

"Like a nail of tenderness": a beautiful simile for God's loving assault on the heart, calling it back to himself.

[4] *The Autobiography of a Thief* (Fox, Duffield, 1903), 83–84. The author describes the experiences of the one he calls "Jim".

[5] *The Portal of the Mystery of Hope*, trans. D.C. Schindler (William B. Eerdmans Publishing, 1996), 93.

Father Sebastian Bowden

To Oscar Wilde, the day after they discussed his life poisoned by "bad influences mental and moral, and by positive sin":

God in his mercy has not let you remain contented in this state. He has proved to you the hollowness of this world ... and has removed thereby a great obstacle to your conversion; He allows you to feel the sting of conscience and the yearnings for a holy, pure, and earnest life. It depends therefore on your own free will which life you will lead. As God calls you, He is bound, remember, to give you the means to obey the call. Do so promptly and cheerfully and difficulties disappear and with your conversion your true happiness would begin.[6]

Servant of God Dorothy Day

Before her conversion:

It was on these cold bitter evenings that I first heard "The Hound of Heaven," in an atmosphere of drink and smoke. Gene [writer Eugene O'Neill] could recite all of Francis Thompson's poem, and would sit there, black and dour, his head sunk as he intoned, "And now my heart is as a broken fount, wherein tear drippings stagnate." The idea of this pursuit by the Hound of Heaven fascinated me. The recurrence of it, the inevitableness of the outcome made me feel that sooner or later I would have to pause in

[6] Quoted in Joseph Pearce, *Literary Converts: Spiritual Inspiration in an Age of Unbelief* (Ignatius Press, 2006), 4.

the mad rush of living and remember my first beginning and my last end.[7]

In Francis Thompson's wonderful poem "The Hound of Heaven", God is the Hound of Heaven ever pursuing his lost children, troubling them, never leaving them in peace, endlessly calling them back. And when the human heart surrenders, it asks with dawning marvel, "Is my gloom after all, shade of his hand outstretched caressingly?" Shade, yes—God's action stings and bites—but only the shade of his hand outstretched caressingly.

[7] *The Long Loneliness* (Harper & Row, 1952), 84. For complementary quotations, see Timothy M. Gallagher, O.M.V., *The Discernment of Spirits: An Ignatian Guide to Everyday Living* (Crossroad, 2005): St. Augustine (27–31); Gallagher, *Setting Captives Free*: Blaise Pascal (13), St. Augustine (13), Thomas Merton (13–14), Alessandro Manzoni (14–15).

Rule 2

If You Are Moving Toward God, Keep Going

In his second rule, Ignatius turns to the much happier situation of persons who do not want sin, whether serious or not, and who seek to grow in the love and service of God. As we would expect, because the person's direction of life is contrary to that described in the first rule, the actions of the two spirits will also be the opposite of their actions recounted in the first rule. In rule 1, the *enemy* seeks to *assist* the movement away from God, and the *good spirit* seeks to *hinder* that movement. Now, when the person is moving toward God, the *enemy* seeks to *hinder* that movement, and the *good spirit* seeks to *assist* it.

Ignatius writes:

> Second Rule. In persons who are going on intensely purifying their sins and rising from good to better in the service of God our Lord, the method is contrary to that in the first rule. For then it is proper to the evil spirit to bite, sadden, and place obstacles, disquieting with false reasons, so that the person may not go forward. And it is proper to the good spirit to give courage and strength, consolations, tears, inspirations and quiet, easing and taking away all obstacles, so that the person may go forward in doing good.

In this rule, Ignatius addresses the blessed situation of people who, with all their human limitations (Prov 24:16), sincerely love the Lord, do not want to sin, and seek to live their vocations well. These are, Ignatius says, "persons who are going on intensely purifying their sins and rising from good to better in the service of God our Lord".

A woman is invited to a weekly Bible study. She has never read the Bible and is intrigued. She registers, attends the weekly sessions, and finds them edifying. Scripture begins to speak to her heart, bringing clarity and a new desire for God. As the Bible is explained, she understands the Eucharist and Confession better and draws closer to them in her daily life. Confession becomes an ongoing practice and helps her identify habits that she now sees as harmful to her relationship with God: certain ways of using the internet, conversations that descend into gossip, and instances of self-centeredness that close her to her family's needs.

She loves this new closeness to God and seeks to remove the obstacles to it. She changes the way she uses the internet, quietly withdraws from harmful conversations, and strives to be more available to her husband and children. She is, Ignatius says, a person who is "going on intensely purifying [her] sins."

Some months later, she attends a Lenten series on prayer. The talks awaken in her a desire for prayer, and, following the counsel of the speaker, she begins to pray daily with Scripture. She also starts listening to a Rosary app when she is alone in the car. Her husband notices that now she smiles more, is more patient with the children, spends more time with them, and is more willing to help. Something warm stirs in the home, and it becomes a happier place. She blesses the Lord for the goodness that has entered her life, and in her prayer, she asks, "Lord, what are the next steps on this path? Where are you calling me to live more deeply my vocation as wife and mother? To serve with greater love in my work and in my life in the Church? Show me how to grow." She is, in Ignatius' words, a person who is "rising from good to better in the service of God our Lord".

When this woman or any of us is growing in like fashion, how will the enemy work to hinder this growth, and how will the good spirit work to assist it? Ignatius addresses these questions in rule 2.

The Hindering Action of the Enemy

Biting

The word used in the original, *morder*—which means "to bite"—indicates that the enemy will bite, gnaw, harass, and diminish the peace and joy these people feel. He will seek to instill a sense of trouble, of disquiet. Consider the following examples:

- "Yes, you did that (took that new step in prayer, in your service of the Lord, in living your vocation, in your love of others, and similar steps), but why did it take you so long?"
- "Yes, you did that, but you know you could have done more."
- "Yes, you did that, but you know it won't last. It never does with you."
- "Yes, you'll grow a little, but not much. You'll always be mediocre."

If people do not recognize this "biting" as the action of the enemy, and if they fail to reject it, then their energy for spiritual growth will diminish—as the enemy desires. If, however, they are *aware* ("Wait a minute"), do *understand* this as a tactic of the enemy ("This isn't right"), and do *take action* to *reject* it ("With God's help, I am going forward on this path"), then not only are they unharmed, but they are also spiritually strengthened. Each time we reject such tactics of the enemy, we grow stronger.

Saddening

This is not the natural sadness one feels, for example, at the loss of a loved one. Such sadness is a sign of a healthy heart that loves. Nothing is healthy about the sadness the enemy induces: a heaviness, a lack of joy, a sense of burden, a loss of energy regarding prayer, the spiritual life, the living of one's vocation, and one's relationship to God in general. Thoughts like these arise in the sadness: "You took that step to grow in your spiritual life, and you felt joy in doing so. Where is that joy today? Where was it in the past days? Now you don't feel any desire for prayer, for a deeper spiritual life. Why continue with all this when there is no joy in it? What is the point of it?" The same observation about unawareness and awareness and the consequences of both applies to this and the following tactics of the enemy.

Placing Obstacles

The enemy instills a feeling that this effort to grow spiritually is too hard, too burdensome, that we are too weak to persevere, to conquer the difficulties that stand in the way. He presents spiritual progress as too difficult: "You want to overcome that issue that holds you back spiritually? You know you can't live without this. You want to take new steps to grow spiritually? How many times have you tried? How long has it ever lasted? What makes you think it will be any different this time? You know yourself. You know you can't take that new step. Try if you want. It may last a week or ten days. But you know it will fall apart. It always does, and it will this time too."

Obstacles, obstacles, obstacles. "It's too difficult. You can't do it. Why make the effort when you know you will fail?"

We need not be ashamed or surprised when we experience these tactics of the enemy. In fact, the enemy employs them precisely when we *are growing spiritually*. This is our universal spiritual experience in a fallen, yes, but redeemed and loved world. What matters is discernment: We must be aware, understand, take action—in this case, to reject.

Disquieting with False Reasons

The enemy will bring "reasons" to discourage this person's growth. As we would expect of the "liar and the father of lies" (Jn 8:44), these "reasons" will be false, and their effect will be to disquiet these persons, to trouble them, to diminish the peace and joy of their spiritual growth. Thus, for example: "Yes, you started praying daily, going to Mass during the week, listening to a Rosary app as you drive. You'd like to think this is because you seek to grow spiritually. You won't admit it, but you know this is really competition with your spouse, with your friend at church. They've always been the spiritual ones. You want people to think you're spiritual too. Something else you won't admit: You want people to see you pray and be impressed."

No such "reasons" were at all present when these persons took that new step. The enemy brings false reasons to trouble them and weaken their resolve. Again, no shame, no surprise: We need only to be aware, understand, take action.

The Assisting Action of the Good Spirit

But a spirit stronger than the enemy is also at work. The good spirit gives the following to strengthen these persons:

Courage and Strength

This is the heartening, uplifting, strengthening action of the good spirit. The good spirit gives courage and strength in endlessly creative ways. For example, a woman will learn the result of the biopsy tomorrow. It is the evening before, and her heart is heavy. What will she hear? What consequences will this have for her? For her family? Some months ago, she began praying the shortened form of Evening Prayer from a monthly publication. She takes the booklet in hand and begins her prayer. When she does, she finds Psalm 27 in the text: "The LORD is my light and my salvation; whom shall I fear? . . . He will hide me in his shelter in the day of trouble; he will conceal me under the cover of his tent, he will set me high upon a rock" (v. 1, 5). When she prays these words, her heart lifts: "Lord, you will be with me tomorrow. Whatever happens, you will be with me and keep me safe." Through a psalm, the good spirit gives this woman "courage and strength".

Consolations

At such times, the heart is warmed with a sense of God's love and presence. Ignatius will discuss consolation in rule 3, and we will return to it in the next chapter.

Tears

The body, too, may participate in the consolation the heart experiences. Ignatius will consider this also in rule 3, and we will examine it there.

Inspirations and Quiet

The enemy brings false reasons—lies—that disquiet. The good spirit gives inspirations that instill quiet—that is, peace—in the heart. Through this action of the good spirit, we perceive with new clarity the way forward on our spiritual journey. At such times, with an uplifted heart we say, "This is the answer. This is what I need to do. This is the next step for growth." Consider the following examples:

- A man hears a homily in which the priest invites his people to pray ten minutes every day with the readings from the day's Mass. As this man listens, he finds himself thinking, "I could do that. I can find the time without difficulty. I can subscribe to a monthly publication with the daily readings. My wife is already doing this. I know she'd be happy to help me begin this practice and answer any questions I may have. I'll subscribe to the publication, talk with my wife, and begin."

- A woman joins the faith-formation group in the parish. In one meeting, the speaker shares her experience of praying with her husband and how this has blessed her marriage. As the woman listens, she wonders whether she and her husband might try this. She knows he would be open to the conversation. She decides to speak with him about this.

Removal of All Obstacles

The enemy places obstacles to hinder the person's progress; the good spirit eases and removes all obstacles so that the person may go forward. Note Ignatius' confidence in the power of the good spirit's action: easing and taking away *all* obstacles. We are never "defeated before we begin"!

The word *all* is powerful here. We may at times have to struggle against obstacles, but *no* obstacle is beyond the power and love of the good spirit. Between an unhappy, discouraged, and passive acceptance of a spiritual obstacle and an active engagement in the struggle to overcome it, with trust in the power of God's grace, the difference is great and blessed. Let's look at these examples of the obstacle-removing action of the good spirit:

- A man sincerely strives to overcome a moral failing. He tries but repeatedly falls. His wife is always present to encourage him. She helps him believe that real progress is possible, and he perseveres. Gradually, this failing diminishes. His wife is an instrument of the good spirit's action, easing and taking away all obstacles.
- A woman has always wanted a daily life of prayer but has never felt able to sustain this. A friend suggests that she read Saint Francis de Sales' *Introduction to the*

Devout Life. She does so, and for the first time, she understands meditation and how to do it. She begins meditation as a daily practice and loves the fruits of it. Saint Francis de Sales' book and her friend who made the suggestion are instruments of the good spirit for this woman, easing and taking away obstacles, opening for her a new life of prayer.

The First Two Rules

Prior to his conversion at age thirty, Ignatius exemplified the profile of rule 1, the persons "going from mortal sin to mortal sin". After his conversion, however, he embodied the profile of rule 2, the persons "who are going on intensely purifying their sins and rising from good to better in the service of God our Lord". He was given grace to describe the actions of the enemy and of the good spirit in both situations, a great blessing for us all.

The enemy's biting is cutting, belittling, harsh, sharp, attacking, accusing. This will never be the Holy Spirit's tone, even when he "stings" our conscience. Such internal stirrings in those who, with their human imperfections, sincerely love the Lord and want to grow in his service are clearly of the enemy and are to be rejected.

Years ago, I was on retreat. When I met with my director on the second day, he helped me see that the struggles I was experiencing in prayer are a normal part of growth, that they can be understood and the way forward clarified. The director also helped me to identify the enemy in the harshness and accusation I was feeling about these struggles. This was the enemy's "biting". To see this and to reject it was liberating.

Witnesses to Rule 2

Reginald Garrigou-Lagrange, O.P.

We should note exactly the different movements of our soul in order to discover what comes from God and what does not. Spiritual writers generally say that God's action in a soul submissive to grace [a rule-2 person] is ordinarily characterized by peace and tranquillity; the devil's action is violent and accompanied by disturbance and anxiety.[1]

Pope Francis

He [Jesus] tells his disciples: "The Holy Spirit, whom the Father will send in my name, *will teach you everything*, and *remind you of all* I have said to you" (Jn 14:26).... The Holy Spirit is an *active* memory; he constantly rekindles the love of God in our hearts. We have experienced his presence in the forgiveness of our sins, in moments when we are filled with his peace, his freedom and his consolation. It is essential to cherish this spiritual memory. We always remember the things that go wrong; we listen to the voice within us that reminds us of our failure and failings, the voice that keeps saying: "Look, yet another failure, yet another disappointment. You will never succeed; you cannot do it". This is a terrible thing to be told. Yet the Holy Spirit tells us something completely different. He reminds us: "Have you fallen? You are a son or daughter of God.

[1] *The Three Ages of the Interior Life: Prelude of Eternal Life*, trans. M. Timothea Doyle, vol. 2 (Catholic Way, 2014), 289.

You are a unique, elect, precious and beloved child. Even when you lose confidence in yourself, God has confidence in you!"[2]

Again the two voices, the discouraging, saddening voice of the enemy, and the encouraging, hope-instilling voice of the good spirit—pure rule 2. Reject the first; accept, believe, drink in, be strengthened by the second.

Saint Ignatius

In a letter to Sister Teresa Rejadell:

[If the enemy] comes upon one whose conscience is delicate (a delicate conscience being in itself nothing faulty, however) and sees that such a person avoids not only all mortal and all venial sin (as much as the latter is possible, for we cannot avoid them all) but even tries to keep from himself the very appearance of slight sin, imperfection, and defect, he tries to darken and confuse that good conscience by suggesting sin where there is none, changing perfection into defect, his only purpose being to harass and make one uneasy and miserable. When, as frequently happens, he cannot induce one to sin, or even hope to do so, he tries at least to vex him.[3]

Both the enemy's biting and disquieting with false reasons are described here. Reject his lies. A blessed liberation of heart follows when we do.

[2] Homily for Pentecost (St. Peter's Basilica, June 5, 2022), https://www.vatican.va/content/francesco/en/homilies/2022/documents/20220605-omelia-pentecoste.html.

[3] *Letters of St. Ignatius of Loyola*, ed. and trans. William J. Young (Loyola University Press, 1959), 21.

Saint Teresa of Avila

Of the false humility instilled by the enemy:

He is recognized clearly by the disturbance and disquiet with which he begins, by the agitation the soul feels as long as his work lasts, by the darkness and affliction he places in the soul, and by dryness and the disinclination toward prayer or toward any good work. It seems that he smothers the soul and binds up the body so that it profits from nothing. Even though the soul knows its own wretchedness and grieves to see what we are,... true humility doesn't come to the soul with agitation or disturbance, nor does it darken it or bring it dryness. Rather, true humility consoles and acts in a completely opposite way: quietly, gently, and with light.[4]

The enemy darkens and afflicts (rule 2, first part); the good spirit consoles, working gently and with light (rule 2, second part).

Saint Thérèse of Lisieux

To her cousin Marie Guérin, regarding Marie's scruples about receiving Holy Communion:

You did well to write me, and I understand *everything* ... *everything, everything, everything*! ...

You haven't committed the shadow of any evil; I know what these kinds of temptations are so well that I can assure

[4] *The Book of Her Life*, in *The Collected Works of St. Teresa of Avila*, trans. Kieran Kavanaugh, O.C.D., and Otilio Rodriguez, O.C.D., vol. 1 (ICS Publications, 1976), 197–98.

you of this without any fear, and, besides, Jesus tells me this in the depth of my heart.... We must despise all these temptations, and pay no attention whatsoever to them.

Should I tell you something that has given me *much* sorrow?

It is that my little Marie has given up her Communions ... on the feast of the Ascension and on the last day of Mary's month! ... Oh, what sorrow this has caused Jesus! ...

The devil has to be very clever to mislead a soul in this way! ... But don't you know, my dear, that this is the only goal of his desires? The evil one knows well that he can't make a soul that wants to belong totally to Jesus commit a sin, so he tries to make the soul believe it has....

Oh, my darling, think, then, that Jesus is there in the Tabernacle expressly for you, for you alone; He is burning with the desire to enter your heart ... so don't listen to the devil, mock him, and go without any fear to receive Jesus in peace and love![5]

Thérèse, here, is an instrument of the good spirit, giving courage and strength, unmasking the enemy's biting, saddening, placing of obstacles, and disquieting with false reasons.

Saint Francis de Sales

[The enemy] makes his ambush in sadness, and then, having troubled the soul with a multitude of sad thoughts cast hither and thither in the understanding, he makes a charge upon the affections, bearing them down with distrust, jealousies, aversions, envies, superfluous apprehensions of past sins, adding withal a number of vain, sour and melancholy

[5] *Saint Thérèse of Lisieux: General Correspondence*, ed. and trans. John Clarke, O.C.D. (ICS Publications, 1982), 567–68.

subtleties of the imagination, that all reasons and consolations may be rejected.[6]

An excellent description of the troubling action of the enemy in one who desires to grow spiritually. Again, be aware, understand, take action (reject).

By inspirations we mean all those interior attractions, motions, acts of self-reproach and remorse, lights and conceptions that God works in us and predisposes our hearts by his blessings, fatherly care, and love in order to awaken, stimulate, urge, and attract us to holy virtues, heavenly love, and good resolutions, in short, to everything that sends us on our way to our everlasting welfare.[7]

The action of the good spirit: bringing inspirations. Accept these and follow where the good spirit leads.

Resolve to accept willingly all the inspirations it may please God to send you. When they come, receive them as ambassadors sent by the King of Heaven who desires to enter into a marriage contract with you. Listen calmly to his proposal, think of the love with which you are inspired, and cherish that holy inspiration. Give it your complete, loving, and permanent consent.[8]

Blessed are those whose hearts are ever open to God's inspirations; they will never lack what they need to live good holy lives, or to perform properly the duties of their state.[9]

A lovely commentary on Ignatius' word accept.

[6] *Treatise on the Love of God*, XXI, https://www.ccel.org/ccel/desales/love.xii.xxi.html.

[7] *Introduction to the Devout Life*, trans. John K. Ryan (Image Books, 1950), 98.

[8] *Introduction to the Devout Life*, 100.

[9] *The Love of God: A Treatise*, trans. Vincent Kerns (Newman Press, 1962), 342.

A Man, Invited to Make a Weekend Retreat

In the days leading up to and on the drive to the weekend, I met with the most serious spiritual desolation I had encountered to date. "You don't want to change your life without thinking this through." "This will put a strain on your job." "This will put a strain on your marriage." "Great, more things on your plate." "You will die at fifty-five at the rate you are going."

On the drive up, I encountered many positive thoughts encouraging me along. "You can do this." "Remember, you said you would attend." "You looked forward to this." I made it there and loved the weekend. It changed my life in ways I had never imagined. After the weekend, I engaged in the post-retreat support activities that held me accountable to a continued life of prayer, study, and evangelization.[10]

His first set of thoughts were classic obstacle-placing action of the enemy: to be rejected. His second set of thoughts were classic action of the good spirit: giving courage and strength. Because the man accepts this grace, great fruit follows.

The Same Man, Years Later, on the Verge of Ordination as a Permanent Deacon

As we got nearer to the day of final decision and then ordination, I had one particularly memorable event. It was Tuesday at work, and out of nowhere came a storm of thoughts. "You are not supposed to do this." "You want this, God does not." "You will be an utter failure." "You will be another one of those clergy who will do damage to

[10] Anonymous personal testimony shared with permission.

the Church." "Your brothers [fellow candidates for diaconal ordination] are putting on an act when they encourage you—they really talk badly about you behind your back." *"Do not do this!"* Needless to say, I thought that maybe all of this was true. I thought back to my Ignatian classes and said, I should not act on these thoughts, and I need to meet with my spiritual advisor.[11]

Again, classic obstacle-placing action of the enemy described very well. The attack passed; the man spoke with his spiritual director about it and was confirmed in his diaconal calling.

Bishop Attila Miklósházy, S.J.

Of the retreat before his priestly ordination:

I was making my retreat in preparation for my ordination to the priesthood, and I was in desolation. I wondered if I even wanted priesthood or if I'd be able to do it. A Jesuit brother in his eighties at that retreat house was an institution. Everyone knew him and loved him for his goodness and kindness. He must have seen the discouragement in this young Jesuit just weeks away from ordination. We were in silence, so he didn't say anything. One day, he simply approached me and handed me a nice red apple. His gesture of kindness changed everything. The desolation left me, and consolation returned.[12]

This brother was an instrument of the good spirit, giving courage and strength, easing and taking away all obstacles.

[11] Shared with permission.

[12] This testimony was shared by Bishop Miklósházy in conversation with the author.

Saint Pierre Favre

One day, on the feast of St. James, as I went to the altar and began Mass, I felt myself in bondage to all my imperfections. And when I began the third versicle, "Why do I walk in sorrow while my enemy afflicts me?" [Ps 43:2] there came to me a thought in the form of a question as if the good spirit were speaking to me thus: "Why be downcast because the enemy afflicts you? If he troubles you, it is because you do not comply with his will."[13]

The good spirit gives Saint Pierre courage and strength. An important point is expressed here: These tactics of the enemy are not pleasant, and we need to reject them. But, as Saint Pierre says, if the enemy brings them, it is only because we do not want sin and want to grow in love and service of God. It is actually a good sign that the enemy attempts these tactics. "If he troubles you, it is because you do not comply with his will."

Saint Faustina Kowalska

O my Jesus, how very easy it is to become holy; all that is needed is a bit of good will. If Jesus sees this little bit of good will in the soul, He hurries to give Himself to the soul, and nothing can stop Him, neither shortcomings nor falls—absolutely nothing. Jesus is anxious to help that soul, and if it is faithful to this grace from God, it can very soon attain the highest holiness possible for a creature here on earth. God is very generous and does not deny His grace to anyone. Indeed He gives more than what we ask of

[13] *The Spiritual Writings of Pierre Favre*, trans. Edmond Murphy, S.J., and Martin Palmer, S.J. (Institute of Jesuit Sources, 1996), 98–99.

Him. *Faithfulness to the inspirations of the Holy Spirit*—that is the shortest route.[14]

Saint John Bosco

Fr Cafasso [the future Saint Joseph Cafasso], who for six years had been my guide, was especially my spiritual director. If I have been able to do any good, I owe it to this worthy priest in whose hands I placed every decision I made, all my study, and every activity of my life. It was he who first took me into the prisons, where I soon learned how great was the malice and misery of mankind. I saw large numbers of young lads aged from 12 to 18, fine healthy youngsters, alert of mind, but seeing them idle there, infested with lice, lacking food for body and soul, horrified me. Public disgrace, family dishonour, and personal shame were personified in those unfortunates. What shocked me most was to see that many of them were released full of good resolutions to go straight, and yet in a short time they landed back in prison, within a few days of their release.

On such occasions I found out how quite a few were brought back to that place; it was because they were abandoned to their own resources. "Who knows?" I thought to myself, "if these youngsters had a friend outside who would take care of them, help them, teach them religion on feast days ... Who knows but they could be steered away from ruin, or at least the number of those who return to prison could be lessened?"

[14] *Divine Mercy in My Soul: The Diary of the Servant of God Sister M. Faustina Kowalska* (Marian Press, 1987), 136–37, emphasis added.

I talked this idea over with Fr Cafasso. With his encouragement and inspiration I began to work out in my mind how to put the idea into practice, leaving to the Lord's grace what the outcome would be.[15]

One man accepts an inspiration of the good spirit—and thousands of young men are blessed. What will happen in your life if you accept the inspirations of the good spirit?

[15] *Memoirs of the Oratory of Saint Francis de Sales: From 1815 to 1855*, trans. Daniel Lyons, S.D.B. (Don Bosco Publications, 1989), 182, ellipses in original. For complementary quotations, see Timothy M. Gallagher, O.M.V., *The Discernment of Spirits: An Ignatian Guide for Everyday Living* (Crossroad, 2005): St. Ignatius (40–41); Timothy M. Gallagher, O.M.V., *Setting Captives Free: Personal Reflections on Ignatian Discernment of Spirits* (Crossroad, 2018): Saint John of the Cross (29).

Rule 3

Recognize Spiritual Consolation

In his third rule, Ignatius turns to those times when our hearts are warmed with a sense of God's love and closeness. Ignatius names this experience "spiritual consolation". In his text, I have highlighted with italics the different forms such consolations may assume.

> Third Rule. The third is of spiritual consolation. I call it consolation when some interior movement is caused in the soul, through which *the soul comes to be inflamed with love of its Creator and Lord*, and, consequently *when it can love no created thing on the face of the earth in itself, but only in the Creator of them all*. Likewise, when it sheds *tears* that move to love of its Lord, whether out of sorrow for one's sins, or for the passion of Christ our Lord, or because of other things directly ordered to his service and praise. Finally, I call consolation *every increase of hope, faith and charity*, and *all interior joy* that calls and attracts to heavenly things and to the salvation of one's soul, quieting it and giving it peace in its Creator and Lord.

"Spiritual consolation". Two words, both significant. *Consolation*: an uplifting movement of the heart—joy, peace, gratitude, love, hope, and similar affective movements. *Spiritual*: on the level of faith, of our relationship with God, of our spiritual lives.

A man is worried about problems at home and at work. He goes to daily Mass this morning. The Gospel is the calming of the storm (Mt 8:23–27). In his homily, the priest speaks of trust in God even in the midst of life's storms, and the man's heart is gently warmed. He feels God's closeness, and hope awakens in his heart that God will guide him through his present problems. This man experiences *spiritual consolation*: an uplifting movement of the heart (hope) on the spiritual level (trust that God will be with him). In theological terms, spiritual consolation is an actual grace: a temporary help given by God to encourage and strengthen us in our spiritual lives.[1]

Consolation may be experienced also on the natural, human, physiological, and psychological level: A woman enjoys a meal with a friend, her husband, or her family; a man exercises and feels his spirits lift; a woman listens to beautiful music and feels more cheerful; a man gazes at the beauty of fall foliage and is uplifted by the sight; a woman works diligently at a project and is happy to see it conclude well and bear fruit. These are the many natural joys that God has built into his creation and that he intends we enjoy. We will call such experiences *nonspiritual consolation*. As the previous examples indicate, there are many healthy nonspiritual consolations.

In his rules, however, Ignatius speaks specifically of *spiritual* consolation. This does not signify that nonspiritual consolation has no importance for the spiritual life. In God's providence, healthy nonspiritual consolation (exercise, an uplifting conversation, the experience of beauty) is often the space into which God infuses the grace of spiritual consolation (a warm sense of his love, his closeness, new courage in the spiritual life).

[1] Timothy M. Gallagher, O.M.V., *Setting Captives Free: Personal Reflections on Ignatian Discernment of Spirits* (Crossroad, 2018), 52–54.

An important corollary follows: A certain amount of healthy nonspiritual consolation is a great blessing not only for our humanity on the natural level but also for our spiritual lives. Much becomes easier in the spiritual life when fitting healthy nonspiritual consolation is present.

Forms of Spiritual Consolation

Ignatius describes spiritual consolation through a list of such experiences. Following his lead, we will review them.

The Soul Inflamed with Love of Its Creator

Saint Thérèse of Lisieux sees a mother hen in the convent garden, her outstretched wings protecting her little chicks. The sight speaks to her of God's faithful love for his people and tells her the story of God's protecting love in her own life. Intense, warm, deep gratitude to God stirs within her, and her tears fall abundantly. Her heart is "inflamed with love of her Creator and Lord".[2]

Raïssa Maritain begins to pray the Litany of the Sacred Heart and never moves beyond the first invocation. Her heart is suddenly filled with a keen sense of the Father's closeness, of his tenderness, of his love for her. Her tears, too, begin to fall. Raïssa's heart is "inflamed with love of its Creator and Lord".[3]

A man spends time with his wife and children. His heart is warmed with gratitude to God for the gift of his family.

Another, in a time of discouragement, prays while meditating on Jesus' encounter with Zacchaeus (Lk 19:1–10).

[2] *St. Thérèse of Lisieux: Her Last Conversations*, trans. John Clarke, O.C.D. (ICS Publications, 1977), 60.

[3] *Raïssa's Journal*, ed. Jacques Maritain (Magi, 1974), 35.

He witnesses the love with which Jesus responds to this disheartened man, and his heart lifts, knowing that Jesus responds in like manner to him this day.

A woman speaks with her daughter in college and rejoices to learn that she has grown closer to the Lord. The mother's heart is enkindled with love for the Lord, who is helping her daughter through a difficult time.

Loving No Created Thing Except in the Creator

A young woman is discerning her vocation. She and a young man have drawn close, and marriage is a real possibility. She also feels a strong attraction to religious life. Pulled both ways, she struggles. In her parish, the Blessed Sacrament is exposed on Saturdays. Today, she spends an hour in Adoration. She gazes at the monstrance on the altar before her. As she does, a deep sense of the Lord's Real Presence before her stirs in her heart, with a profound, warm sense of the Lord's love for her. In that moment, she finds herself saying to the Lord, with no struggle at all, "Whatever you want, Lord. If you want me to be married, I'll be married. If you want me to be a religious, I'll be a religious."

The woman experiences a second form of spiritual consolation. This may be given when the heart is "inflamed with love of its Creator and Lord" and is thereby set free to love all created things—occupations, possessions, places, relationships—"in the Creator of them all". When blessed with such consolation, the tension we may feel between God's leading and other attractions to created things disappears. We find ourselves free to love these created gifts in the richest and most fruitful way—that is, in accordance with God's plan for our lives.

Tears of Love, Remorse, or Sorrow

A woman waits in line for Confession. The Confession will not be easy because she has difficult things to say. Her turn arrives, and, with some struggle, she says all that she needs to say. The priest's words lighten her burden, and when she receives absolution, the weight on her heart lifts completely. Tears of consolation come to her eyes.

Trouble has arisen at work, and a man is anxious. He prays daily with the readings of the Mass, and today's Gospel is the encounter of the risen Lord with his disciples, who have locked themselves in a room out of fear (Jn 20:19–23). The man sees Jesus approach them and repeat twice, "Peace be with you." He witnesses their joy when they grasp that Good Friday was not the end, that the Lord has conquered death, and that he is with them. As the man prays, the beginning of a tear comes to his eye. "You are with me, too, Lord. You will see me through."

Here Ignatius indicates that the body also may participate in the grace of spiritual consolation.

Increase of Hope

Three months ago, a woman began to dedicate twenty minutes to prayer each morning. She found this fruitful and loved the difference it made in her day. Recently, her prayer has been dry, and it has been hard to persevere.

Today, the Gospel is the encounter of Jesus and Bartimaeus. The woman begins her prayer, fully committed to the twenty minutes but expecting that the prayer will be as dry as in the preceding days. She reads through the passage slowly, but nothing strikes her. She reads it a second time, and now the words "Take courage; get up, he is calling you" speak to her heart (Mk 10:46–52, NABRE). She senses that the Lord is with her and is inviting her, too, to take courage. She says to the Lord, "Jesus, I'm glad that I am here today. You may have more yet to give me in this time of prayer." The woman experiences the increase of hope that is spiritual consolation.

A man arrives for a weekend retreat, faithful to the commitment he made but feeling that little will come of these days. At dinner the first evening, he meets another retreatant and enjoys an uplifting conversation about spiritual matters. He finds himself saying to the Lord, "Jesus, thank you for bringing me here. I'm sure that you have grace in store for me this weekend." This man also experiences the increase of hope that is spiritual consolation.

Increase of Faith

A man goes to daily Mass. He understands and believes the Church's teaching on the Mass. Today, at the moment of Consecration, his faith in the Real Presence of Jesus in the transubstantiated Bread and Wine is particularly alive. He feels this truth in a special way, and his heart lifts as the priest proclaims the words and elevates the Bread and Wine.

A woman is reading John 14, Jesus' words to his disciples on Holy Thursday: "Let not your hearts be troubled.... I am the way, and the truth, and the life.... If you ask anything in my name, I will do it" (vv. 1, 6, 14). As she reads, she senses that this is the Word of God to her today, living, full of love, personally directed to her. She feels God's closeness as his Word touches her heart.

A man attends the Baptism of a friend's baby. He watches and listens as the rite unfolds: the readings, the prayers, the

Baptism itself, the anointings, the candle. As he does, the reality of his own Baptism awakens in a fresh way for him: He has been *baptized*; he is a son of God, saved from original sin, a member of the Church, and free to pursue eternal life. Gratitude stirs in his heart with a resolve to explore Baptism more deeply.

Such experiences exemplify the increase of faith that Ignatius calls spiritual consolation. This consolation is not a movement from unbelief to belief but a felt, warm, uplifting increase in a faith already accepted. Like all spiritual consolation, the increase of faith endures for a time and then, as is true of actual grace, gently passes. But it leaves its blessing.

Increase of Charity

After the Mass in which his faith was so alive, the man remains in church for some minutes of prayer. His heart is warmed by the gift given in the Mass and the reception of Holy Communion. He rises from the pew, walks to his car, and drives to work, all the while feeling God's love in his heart. He knows that he is ready to face the day with the love received from God. In that love, he is prepared to respond to others with a smile and willingness to help.

A woman rises from her morning prayer. She has prayed with Saint Paul's words, "I live, no longer I, but Christ lives in me; insofar as I now live in the flesh, I live by faith in the Son of God who has loved me and given himself up for me" (Gal 2:20, NABRE). The words "who has loved *me*", said in the singular, spoke deeply to her of God's personal love for her, and her heart lifted in gratitude to him. As she begins her duties today, she knows she is ready to engage her family with love.

Interior Joy That Gives Peace

Interior (spiritual) joy manifests as an attraction to "heavenly things" (prayer, love of God, Mass, Eucharistic Adoration, love of Mary, the living of one's vocation, holiness) and to eternal life, a stilling of the heart, and peace in the Lord. In times of such joy, the heart is drawn to the things of God and experiences a deep peace (Jn 14:27).

A man makes a grace-filled retreat and experiences new desire for prayer, for the living of his vocation as husband and father, and for growth in his spiritual life. A woman goes to daily Mass. Today the readings and the homily speak to an anxious place in her heart, remove the burden, and give her joy. She seeks to live her day as a response of love to God and looks forward to attending Mass the next day.

Such is spiritual consolation in its various forms. The blessing of consolation for the spiritual life is evident. Ignatius writes, "It does not remain with us always, but it will always accompany us on the way at the times that God designates. All this is for our progress."[4]

Witnesses to Rule 3

Reginald Garrigou-Lagrange, O.P.

Let us note that the sadness of true contrition, that is, displeasure with evil and detestation of it, is never a vexing, fretful sadness which depresses, but, on the contrary, it is a holy sadness that makes the soul prompt and diligent, that uplifts the heart by prayer and hope, that leads it to

[4] *Letters of St. Ignatius of Loyola*, ed. and trans. William J. Young, S.J. (Loyola University Press, 1959), 22.

outbursts of fervor: "It is a sadness which in the height of its bitterness always produces the sweetness of an incomparable consolation, according to the precept of the great St. Augustine: 'The penitent should ever grieve and rejoice at his grief.' "[5]

A spiritually consoling "sorrow for one's sins" (rule 3).

Saint Ignatius of Loyola

In a letter to Sister Teresa Rejadell:

The first [lesson] is an interior consolation that casts out all uneasiness and draws one to a complete love of our Lord. In this consolation, he enlightens some, and to others he reveals many secrets as a preparation for later visits. In a word, when this divine consolation is present all trials are pleasant and all weariness rest. He who goes forward with this fervor, warmth, and interior consolation finds every burden light and sweetness in every penance or trial, however great. This consolation points out and opens up the way we are to follow and points out the way we are to avoid.[6]

The grace of spiritual consolation brings love for God, clarity, and energy for spiritual things: blessed gifts from God.

The Pilgrim, Narrator of The Way of a Pilgrim

I began to have from time to time a number of different feelings in my heart and mind. Sometimes my heart would

[5] *The Three Ages of the Interior Life: Prelude of Eternal Life*, trans. M. Timothea Doyle, vol. 1 (Catholic Way, 2014), 405.

[6] *Letters*, 21–22.

feel as though it were filled with joy, such light, freedom and consolation were in it. Sometimes I felt a burning love for Jesus Christ and for all God's creatures. Sometimes my eyes brimmed over with tears of thankfulness to God, who was so merciful to me, a wretched sinner. Sometimes my understanding, which had been so stupid before, was given so much light that I could easily grasp and dwell upon matters of which up to now I had not been able even to think at all. Sometimes that sense of a warm gladness in my heart spread throughout my whole being, and I was deeply moved as the fact of the presence of God everywhere was brought home to me. Sometimes by calling upon the Name of Jesus I was overwhelmed with bliss, and now I knew the meaning of the words "*The Kingdom of God is within you* [Lk 17:21]."[7]

Holy ground in this man's heart—beautiful experiences of spiritual consolation as he seeks deeper prayer: joy, light, burning love for Jesus, tears, warm gladness of the heart. The specifically spiritual nature of the consolation is evident: All is on the level of faith, of his relationship with God.

Saint Pierre Favre

On celebrating the first of three Masses on Christmas:

At the first Mass, when I was feeling cold before Communion and was grieved that my dwelling was not better prepared, there came to me a somewhat lively spiritual movement. In it, I received this answer accompanied by an interior feeling of devotion that moved me to tears: "This is what the coming of Christ into a stable means. If you were

[7] *The Way of a Pilgrim and The Pilgrim Continues His Way*, trans. R. M. French (Ballantine Books, 1974), 31.

already very fervent, you would not see here the humanity of your Lord because spiritually you would correspond less to what is called a stable." So I felt consoled in the Lord.[8]

Blessed tears of spiritual consolation.

Saint Teresa of Calcutta

In a letter:

I am on my way back from Manila where I have opened a novitiate.... Then on the night of the 2nd Feb. we had a five days retreat.—The priest cleaned our souls from all sin—and then gave only Jesus.—The day of the confession I told all my sins—and Jesus took all my sins.—After confession I heard my heart singing—Thank you, Jesus, for taking my sins. He really just took them all away.[9]

"After confession I heard my heart singing": holy ground in the heart and a lovely description of spiritual consolation.

Erin Bozeman

After the death of her son:

On this one particularly rough night as I lay in bed sobbing to my husband that I couldn't go on any longer, I briefly opened my eyes to see he was praying over me. I quickly closed them again and just let him continue. It was at this very moment that I felt a peace descend upon me. It was

[8] *The Spiritual Writings of Pierre Favre*, trans. Edmond Murphy, S.J., and Martin Palmer, S.J. (Institute of Jesuit Sources, 1996), 184.

[9] *Mother Teresa: Come Be My Light; The Private Writings of the "Saint of Calcutta"*, ed. Brian Kolodiejchuk, M.C. (Image Books, 2007), 283–84, punctuation in original.

like Jesus laid a warm blanket of comfort over me. It was then I knew I would not have to travel this road alone, and that when I needed him most, he would be there to hold me up.[10]

"Every increase of hope" (rule 3).

William Kernan

From his conversion story, on leaving home in California for college:

I looked out of the train window to the California countryside that I was rapidly leaving behind me—the orange groves shimmering in the light of the late afternoon sun, the little bungalows that appeared here and there for a moment and then were gone as the train sped on, and the mountains far out on the horizon.... An upsurge of gratitude swept through me and warmed my heart, and I thanked God for his providence and goodness that had kept me all the days of my life and which, I was sure, would keep me safe forever. I could go on thinking of tomorrow in terms of today. Something would always be the same in every tomorrow; something would be certain—God.[11]

"Every increase of hope" (rule 3).

James Matthew Wilson (Catholic Poet)

While still a student, I wavered in my faith. But one day at Mass, at the moment I received the Eucharist, I received

[10] Quoted in Dynamic Catholic, *Why I Love Being Catholic: Dynamic Catholic Ambassadors Share Their Hopes and Dreams for the Future* (Wellspring, 2018), 108.

[11] William C. Kernan, *My Road to Certainty* (D. McKay, 1953), 38.

such an overwhelming act of grace, such a flood of it, manifesting to me the reality of the Sacrament that I never again could doubt. It was a confirmation of its reality, such that I understood my own personal feelings had nothing to do with anything. It was knowledge rather than a feeling, and of course knowledge has a kind of stability despite whatever our feelings happen to be at one moment or another.[12]

The "increase of faith" that is a blessed experience of spiritual consolation. Elsewhere, Ignatius speaks of spiritual consolation as "a raising up of the mind".[13]

Servant of God Dorothy Day

Notes from a retreat: One time I was traveling, far from home and lonely, and I awoke in the night almost on the verge of weeping with a sense of futility, of being unloved and unwanted. And suddenly the thought came to me of my importance as a daughter of God, daughter of a King, and I felt a sureness of God's love and at the same time a conviction that one of the greatest injustices (if one can put it that way) which one can do to God is to distrust His love, not realize His love. God so loved me that He gave His only begotten Son. "If a mother will forget her children, never will I forget thee." Such tenderness.[14]

Spiritual consolation as an "increase of love", with a joyful uplift of heart.

[12] Roseanne T. Sullivan, "The Emerging Catholic Literary Renaissance: An Interview with Poet James Matthew Wilson", *Latin Mass* (Christmas 2020): 63, https://www.jamesmatthewwilson.com/uploads/5/1/9/8/51987935/latin_mass_magazine_interview_with_roseanne_sullivan.pdf.

[13] "Autograph Directory of Saint Ignatius Loyola", 11, in *Directoria Exercitiorum Spiritualium (1540–1599)*, ed. Ignacio Iparraguirre, S.J. (Monumenta Historica Societatis Jesu, 1955), 72, author's translation.

[14] *By Little and Little: The Selected Writings of Dorothy Day*, ed. Robert Ellsberg (Alfred A. Knopf, 1983), 219.

Walter Hilton (Fourteenth-Century English Augustinian Writer)

Sometimes a man or woman meditating on God feels a fervor of love and spiritual sweetness in the remembrance of his passion, or any of his works in his humanity; or he feels great trust in the goodness and mercy of God for the forgiveness of his sins, and for his great gifts of grace; ... or else in prayer he feels the thought of his heart draw up from all earthly things, streamed together with all its powers as it rises into our Lord by fervent desire and with spiritual delight.... It seems to him for the time that nothing pleases him so much as praying or thinking as he does for the savor, delight and comfort that he finds in it.[15]

The rich workings of the grace of spiritual consolation.

Michael Jacobs

On a retreat experience:

I went on a retreat my freshman year of high school. On that retreat I heard the Gospel message for the first time. I learned that God loved me personally and desired a personal relationship with me. There was confession and Adoration during Saturday night of the retreat. After going to confession and receiving God's unconditional love and mercy, I knelt before the Eucharist. Looking up at the Host I encountered a peace and joy I'd never experienced before. At that moment, I knew that Jesus

[15] *Walter Hilton: The Scale of Perfection*, trans. John P. H. Clark and Rosemary Dorward (Paulist Press, 1991), 80.

loved me personally, and desired to have a relationship with me.[16]

Again, the blessed fruit, the strengthening, of spiritual consolation.

Saint Charles of Sezze

When I was about seventeen our Lord willed to grant me a very fervent resolve to abandon sin and myself entirely, and follow him who is really the way of truth and life eternal. This inflamed me completely with a love of him and with a longing to do great and generous things in his holy service.... When I began to taste God in prayer and in the reception of the most Blessed Sacrament, my heart was set on fire more intensely and I was moved with pity and compassion toward the poor. I was kind toward everyone and I tried to take care of everyone's needs without considering that thereby I would have to do without something myself. Our Lord joined faith and hope to my charity and I firmly believed and trusted that he would be my sure provider.[17]

Pope Francis

Every Christian, especially you and I, is called to be a bearer of this message of hope that gives serenity and joy: God's consolation, his tenderness toward all. But if we first experience the joy of being consoled by him, of being loved by him, then we can bring that joy to others. This

[16] Quoted in Dynamic Catholic, *Why I Love Being Catholic*, 118.

[17] *St. Charles of Sezze: Autobiography*, ed. and trans. Leonard Perotti, O.F.M. (Burns & Oates, 1963), 13, 18.

is important if our mission is to be fruitful: to feel God's consolation and to pass it on to others! Isaiah's invitation must resound in our hearts: "Comfort, comfort my people" (40:1), and it must lead to mission.[18]

A mission for us all: "to feel God's consolation and to pass it on to others".

[18] Homily (St. Peter's Basilica, July 7, 2013), https://www.vatican.va/content/francesco/en/homilies/2013/documents/papa-francesco_20130707_omelia-seminaristi-novizie.html. For complementary quotations, see Timothy M. Gallagher, O.M.V., *The Discernment of Spirits: An Ignatian Guide for Everyday Living* (Crossroad, 2005): Raïssa Maritain (47), St. Thérèse of Lisieux (49–50); Timothy M. Gallagher, O.M.V., *Setting Captives Free: Personal Reflections on Ignatian Discernment of Spirits* (Crossroad, 2018): Ronald Knox (61).

Rule 4

Recognize Spiritual Desolation

In his fourth rule, Ignatius turns to the contrary of spiritual consolation—that is, spiritual desolation. In such times, our hearts do not feel God's closeness and love, prayer attracts us less or not at all, our energy for spiritual growth wanes, and we feel the attraction of spiritually harmful practices. Awareness, understanding, and knowledge of how to respond to spiritual desolation is Ignatius' primary focus in this and the following ten rules.

Clearly, accepting God's work in spiritual consolation is more important than rejecting the spiritual desolation through which the enemy seeks to undermine that work. Opening our hearts to the grace of spiritual consolation is primary in the discerning life. Ignatius addresses times of spiritual consolation in rules 10 and 11.

But most of us experience fewer problems in accepting spiritual consolation than in rejecting spiritual desolation. For that reason, Ignatius, who is eminently practical, dedicates the majority of his rules to assisting us where we need the most help: identifying and overcoming spiritual desolation.[1]

[1] This situation changes in the setting of Ignatius' Second Rules for discernment. Here, we are concerned with the more common experience described in his First Rules.

In forty years of sharing these rules, I have seen that for most dedicated people (likely any reader of this book) the main obstacle on the spiritual journey is spiritual desolation—that is, those times when we grow discouraged and disheartened in our spiritual lives. If we do not recognize and reject spiritual desolation, it will harm us, as the enemy intends. When this happens, we lose heart and regress.

The troubling state of our world today has increased our vulnerability to desolation. I could not have foreseen forty years ago how increasingly important Ignatius' teaching on spiritual desolation would become.

If, however, we *do* recognize and reject spiritual desolation, not only will it not harm us, but each time we do so, we will grow stronger in the spiritual life. Ignatius composed his fourteen rules precisely to this end.

As with rule 3, I have used italics to highlight the experiences that Ignatius identifies as desolation:

> Fourth Rule. The fourth is of spiritual desolation. I call desolation all the contrary of the third rule, such as *darkness of soul, disturbance in it, movement to low and earthly things, disquiet from various agitations and temptations*, moving to *lack of confidence, without hope, without love*, finding oneself *totally slothful, tepid, sad*, and *as if separated from one's Creator and Lord*. For just as consolation is contrary to desolation, in the same way the thoughts that come from consolation are contrary to the thoughts that come from desolation.

"Spiritual desolation". Again, two words, both significant. *Desolation*: a heavy movement of the heart—discouragement, sadness, anxiety, hopelessness, and similar movements. *Spiritual*: on the level of faith, of our relationship with God, and of our spiritual lives.

Consider how this discouragement plays out in daily life: Last evening, a husband and wife had a tense conversation that did not resolve well. The wife's sleep was troubled, and she found work difficult this morning. Normally, she listens to a prayer app as she drives home from work, but today she felt no desire to do so and did not. In an hour, she will bring the children home from school. This is her quiet time for prayer with Scripture, and generally she welcomes it. But today, prayer does not attract her. She feels neither God's closeness nor his love. Nothing in her wants to open the Bible. Instead, she is drawn to the phone and social media in a way that she knows will not be good. This woman experiences *spiritual desolation*: heavy movements of the heart (discouragement, trouble of heart) on the spiritual level (sense of distance from God, lack of desire for prayer, attraction to spiritually harmful things).

Desolation, like consolation, may be experienced on the natural, human, physiological, and psychological level: A man drives himself excessively at work and sleeps too little, and a heaviness enters his days. A woman receives negative feedback at work, and she feels discouraged. A man disappoints his friend, and this friend is saddened. We will call such experiences *nonspiritual desolation*.

A certain amount of nonspiritual desolation is normal and may even be holy in a well-lived life. A mother stays up several nights in a row with her child who is ill. She grows tired, but there is something holy about that tiredness, embraced out of love for her child and her vocation as mother. A priest guides his parish through Holy Week and is tired. Again, there is something holy about that tiredness, embraced out of love for his people and his calling as a priest. The tiredness of both mother and priest is blessed, though both will need healthy ways to recover their energy.

In his rules, Ignatius speaks specifically of *spiritual* desolation. As with consolation, this does not mean that nonspiritual desolation has no significance for the spiritual life. Very often, nonspiritual desolation—when we feel physically worn or emotionally depressed—is the space into which the enemy brings the further trap of spiritual desolation. Nonspiritual vulnerabilities (physical tiredness, emotional depression), especially when these are substantial and persistent, are a liability not only on the nonspiritual level but on the spiritual level as well: They render us more susceptible to spiritual desolation.

Saint Teresa of Avila, reflecting on bodily indispositions and the life of prayer, writes, "At such times the soul must render the body a service for the love of God, so that on many other occasions the body may render services to the soul."[2] At such times, we must "render services" to—take care of—the body *for the love of God*. Proper care of the body is important for the spiritual life. Many problems that we consider spiritual—they will become spiritual if we do not address them—cease when we pay wise attention to physical and emotional needs. Consider: A man feels that he cannot pray today. He exercises in his habitual way, and now he feels fully ready to pray. The problem was not spiritual in origin but rather nonspiritual: the need to address a physical deficit.

Once more, an important corollary follows: Wise care of our humanity on the nonspiritual level greatly facilitates the spiritual life—in this case, overcoming spiritual desolation. Proper nutrition, sleep, exercise, and healthy recreation diminish our vulnerability to spiritual desolation and so facilitate the struggle against it.

Forms of Spiritual Desolation

Ignatius describes spiritual desolation, like spiritual consolation, through a list of such experiences. He writes, "I call desolation all the contrary of the third rule." Spiritual

[2] *The Life of Teresa of Avila*, trans. E. Allison Peers (Image Books, 1960), 133.

desolation is entirely the *contrary*, the opposite of spiritual consolation. The exact contrariety of these two spiritual movements, for one who attentively lives the discerning life, greatly facilitates the understanding (be aware, *understand*, take action) that permits the appropriate response to both: accepting spiritual consolation and rejecting spiritual desolation. The list follows.

Darkness of Soul

This darkness manifests as confusion, the inability to see clearly in the spiritual life, and a heavy sensation that things are going badly and are likely to worsen. Consider a woman who felt joy and new closeness to God in the weeks after a grace-filled retreat. Now, however, a certain perplexity and darkness burden her spiritual life. Everything feels confused, and she begins to doubt the grace of the retreat. If she is not discerning, this tactic of the enemy will induce regression in her spiritual life. The same holds true for each of us.

Disturbance in the Soul

In this form of spiritual desolation, peace is absent and is replaced by unrest and turmoil of heart. The woman also finds that she has lost the peace she felt after the retreat. Now her heart is troubled and unsettled. If she identifies her loss of peace as the enemy's effort to hinder her new growth, and if she rejects this desolation, no harm will come to her. On the contrary, she will grow stronger against future attacks of the enemy. If she is not discerning, she may find herself thinking, "Well, it was nice for a few weeks, but you're still you. Nothing has really changed."

Should she believe this, her energy for spiritual progress will wane—as the enemy desires.

Movement to Low and Earthly Things

In the joy of spiritual consolation, we are drawn upward toward "heavenly things". As we would expect, the contrary will be true in spiritual desolation. Now the pull is downward toward "low and earthly things". This is when we are drawn to the refrigerator—again; when we incline to the smartphone, and one touch becomes one hundred, becomes two hundred, leading us in a direction where we should not go ... In spiritual desolation, we feel the enticement of these and perhaps worse self-indulgences. The different "low and earthly things" that may appeal in spiritual desolation are not difficult to imagine.

There is no shame in feeling this movement toward low and earthly things. It is simply a tactic of the enemy. That we experience it is, as we have said, even a good sign: Precisely because we are progressing toward God, the enemy attempts to hinder that progress. Obviously, if we give in to this movement, harm will result. But if we are aware, understand this for the tactic of the enemy that it is, and reject it, we will be strengthened spiritually.

Disquiet from Agitations and Temptations

Again, trouble of heart, disquiet, agitation, loss of peace. Ignatius alerts us that in spiritual desolation, the other garden-variety tactic of the enemy will be present: temptations—that is, deceptive suggestions: "Why don't you put off your prayer till later?" "You can let yourself see, have, do that ... It doesn't have to get too far out of hand." Garden-variety does not mean harmless. Obviously, if we give in to spiritual desolation and temptation, we will be harmed, sometimes even greatly, in the spiritual life. Garden-variety signifies that these two tactics, spiritual desolation and temptation, are universal and undramatic. They are the ongoing tactics of the enemy in a spiritual life lived in a fallen, yes, but redeemed and loved world.

Lack of Confidence

This is a cruel tactic of the "liar and the father of lies" (Jn 8:44):

- "You want to grow spiritually? You think your efforts will make a difference? Try, if you want. You'll never change. You'll never grow. You are you, and that's all you'll ever be."
- "You can make all the resolutions you want. They won't change anything. You'll never be much of a (fill in the blank: father, husband, wife, mother, priest, religious, single person, person of prayer, disciple of Jesus). You'll always be mediocre at best, and that's all you can hope for."
- "Try. Try again. Pray. Read the Bible. Go to daily Mass. Join the Bible study. You know you're going to fail, as you always do. It's never lasted before, and it never will. Why do you persist when you know it's going nowhere?"
- "Others, yes, but not you. Why do you keep hoping for a holiness, a living of your vocation, that you will never reach?"

If we believe the voice of desolation, we are likely to succumb and settle unhappily for less. None of this is true!

"I can do all things in him who strengthens me" (Phil 4:13). This is the truth: With the power of God's grace, the growth we seek is possible. Yes, this growth may require effort, and yes, there will be struggles along the way. But there is a world of difference between an undiscerning, hopeless acceptance of such lies and a hope-filled pursuit of growth with confidence in God's grace.

Without Hope

A further cruel lie of the enemy often manifests in the following ways:

- "Go to your time of prayer, if you want. Nothing will come of it. It will be dry, empty, and fruitless. Your prayer today won't be worth much."
- "Go ahead—sign up for that retreat. You think that it will make a difference, that you'll be strengthened in your spiritual life because of it. You're deluding yourself. A few days won't change anything. Maybe things will be different for a few days or a few weeks. But then it will all fall apart and you'll be the same. Why even think of going when there's no point?"
- "You like the idea of the faith-formation class in the parish. You think that you'll learn more about your faith, that you'll meet people with whom to share your spiritual life. It's just one more thing when you're already too busy. You'll get there tired, you won't want to do the readings, and you won't learn much. You might as well just let it go."

This form of spiritual desolation attempts to undermine any hope in spiritual practices and new steps in the spiritual life. Once more, if we are not aware, do not understand, and do not reject these lies of the enemy, they will impede our spiritual growth.

Without Love

This is the opposite of "inflamed with love" when in spiritual consolation. At such times, we do not feel God's love or any sense of love for others in God. Our hearts feel "cold", without love. This signifies neither that God does not love us nor that we do not love God. It does mean that the affective sense of this love—the sense of warmth, of closeness—is absent, having been replaced by a sense of emptiness, of coldness. The same counsel applies.

Totally Slothful

We feel no energy for prayer, for service of the Lord, for participation in parish events, for Mass, for Eucharistic Adoration, for faith-formation classes, or for living our vocation in the family and at work with greater holiness. In this regard, we feel totally—a powerful adverb—slothful, languid, lethargic.

Totally Tepid

In such desolation, we feel no fervor toward spiritual things and their practice. The priest has no desire to prepare his homily, the layperson to attend the parish event, the religious to teach her class, or any of us to pray. We feel totally tepid, listless, unenthusiastic.

Totally Sad

The spiritual joy of consolation is absent and replaced by its contrary. A gray film pervades the spiritual life, a heaviness that may not prevent fidelity to its practices but does weigh upon them. We feel totally sad, unhappy, downcast. In its more substantial form, this sadness—if not discerned—may cause regression.

Feeling As If We Are Separated from God

The person feels, "I'm here, Lord, but you are a million miles away." Ignatius advisedly says "as if" because the truth is that God is Emmanuel (Mt 1:23), with us to the close of the age (Mt 28:20), or, as Saint Augustine says, "more intimate to me than I am to myself".[3] In this form of spiritual desolation, however, the feeling is that "I am alone" and that "you are far away." Again, if not discerned, this sense of distance from God will harm us.

Thoughts That Run Against Consolation

After this list, Ignatius adds a key observation about both spiritual consolation and spiritual desolation. These are, as we have said, affective realities. We experience them on the level of the heart: uplifting or heavy movements of the heart, respectively.

But when we are in spiritual consolation or spiritual desolation, something is also happening on the cognitive

[3] The original phrase is "interior intimo meo", *Confessions* 3, author's translation.

level, in our minds. *Thoughts arise* from both uplifting spiritual consolation and discouraging spiritual desolation. And just as consolation and desolation are contrary affective experiences, so, too, the thoughts that arise from the one and the other are contrary.

A woman undergoes a difficult experience, knows that she needs God, and returns to the practice of her faith. Six months have passed, and she loves the new peace and strength she feels.

This Sunday, she is at Mass, and the Gospel is Luke 11:1–11: "Lord, teach us to pray" (v. 1). The priest gives a heartfelt homily, inviting his parishioners to pray daily with the readings of the Mass. As she listens, the woman feels her heart lift in gratitude to God for the new peace and joy in her life. Her heart warms as she feels God's closeness and love for her. A thought comes: "If just returning to Sunday Mass has made this difference, what would happen if I were to do what Father suggests? I could easily find a few minutes each morning for this prayer. And I have a friend who has done this for years. If I ask her help to get started, she'll be happy to assist me. This evening, when the children are settled, I'll call her and start tomorrow."

Home from Mass, the woman finds an email from a colleague at work who criticizes her contribution to a project they share. Knowing she will need to address this on Monday dampens the joy of her Sunday morning. At supper, a tense conversation with her teenage daughter does not resolve well. This, too, weighs on the woman. The conversation is one more sign of the strain in their relationship.

Now it is evening, the children are settled, and the house is quiet. She remembers that she planned to call her friend at this time and begin her practice of prayer the next morning. The joy and feeling of God's love she experienced that morning have vanished. She feels no energy for spiritual things, for new steps in prayer. Thoughts arise: "Who are you kidding? You've never picked up a Bible in your life. You won't even understand it. And you don't know anything about prayer. What makes you think you'll be able to pray with the Bible? You know yourself. You get these enthusiasms, but they never last. What's the point of calling your friend? She'll get excited to see you taking this new step, and then you'll both be embarrassed when it falls apart in a week or two. You'd better just stay as you are."

Thoughts arise in spiritual consolation as the woman listens to the homily, encouraging thoughts that open a new spiritual path. Thoughts also arise in the spiritual desolation of that evening, discouraging thoughts that seek to impede this new step. Ignatius highlights the exact contrariety of the two sets of thoughts. In terms of discernment—be aware, understand, take action (accept/reject)—the first set of thoughts is to be accepted and the second firmly rejected. If the woman is discerning, she knows she should accept the thoughts arising from spiritual consolation and reject those arising from spiritual desolation: She should call her friend and begin her prayer with Scripture the next morning.

A practical observation follows. To know when we are in spiritual consolation or spiritual desolation brings great clarity into what may otherwise be a confusing, contrasting clamor of thoughts—a clarity that permits progress in the spiritual life.

Spiritual Consolation and Spiritual Desolation

We will complete our discussion of spiritual consolation and spiritual desolation with a review of fundamental truths regarding them. We will also review the qualities of spiritual desolation.

God Gives Spiritual Consolation—Spiritual Desolation Is Always the Work of the Enemy

In the experience described in these fourteen rules, spiritual consolation is always the work of God. It is a grace given to assist us on the spiritual journey. Our part is to live in such a way that our hearts are disposed (Ignatius' word)[4] to receive this grace and, when given, to accept it and allow God to strengthen us through it.

God never gives spiritual desolation. With its discouraging lies, it is always and only the work of the enemy. God permits the enemy to visit us at times with spiritual desolation for reasons of a love that Ignatius addresses in rule 9. Essentially, if we are discerning, if we resist and reject spiritual desolation, we grow in key ways in the spiritual life.

Because spiritual desolation is a work of the enemy, in every case the only right response is to reject it. Ignatius' word for "reject", *lanzar*, means "to thrust" it with energy from us.

Spiritual Consolation Does Not Remain with Us Always

Spiritual consolation is an actual grace. Such graces are temporary aids that God gives to assist us in the spiritual life.[5] They pass but leave their blessing.

[4] See, among many other references, *SpirEx* 1, 7, 20, 135, 213.

[5] *Catechism of the Catholic Church*, nos. 2000, 2024.

Thus, if there is no shame in experiencing spiritual desolation, there is also no shame in not always experiencing spiritual consolation. Ignatius adds that spiritual consolation "will always accompany us on the way at the times God designates".[6]

Spiritual Desolation, Unresisted, Grows

If we do not resist and reject spiritual desolation, it will extend over time and increase in intensity. Undiscerned and unresisted desolation persists: One day of desolation becomes two, becomes a week, and may, unhappily, become months and years. It likewise deepens: A vague discouragement becomes, by degrees, a substantial discouragement and can lead, again if unresisted, to complete loss of hope and energy in the spiritual life. Unresisted spiritual desolation ultimately brings one to "a state of general discouragement".[7] Once there, a person is prone to making decisions that will harm his spiritual life. Ultimately, the desolation will attack the person's vocation.

None of this need happen. The primary thrust of Ignatius' rules is to help us avoid such discouragement and its harmful effects.

Spiritual Desolation, Unresisted, Claims Power over Our Spiritual Past and Future

If undiscerned and unresisted, spiritual desolation will (falsely) claim power to interpret our spiritual past and predict our

[6] *Letters of St. Ignatius of Loyola*, ed. and trans. William J. Young, S.J. (Loyola University Press, 1959), 22.

[7] *Letters*, 22.

spiritual future, always in a dark key. The outlook will be some version of the following: "Look at you this evening. You have no desire to pray. You don't feel God's closeness. All that energy you had for spiritual things is gone, and you are attracted to 'low and earthly things'. You're not much of a spiritual figure. And you know what? You never have been (interpretation of the person's spiritual past) and you never will be (prediction of the person's spiritual future)." If people believe this dark reading of their spiritual past and future, the desolation will grow heavier and they are likely to regress spiritually. The importance of unmasking this lie is evident. As Ignatius writes, "For this reason it is necessary for us *to be aware* of our opponent."[8]

Spiritual Desolation Presents Itself as Our Spiritual Identity

The desolation (enemy) tells you that what you are experiencing (spiritual desolation) is *who you are* spiritually (spiritual identity). You feel little desire for prayer today, and the desolation says, "Do you see who you are? You are a person who does not love prayer." You feel far from God today, and the desolation says, "Do you see who you are? You are a person who *is* far from God." You often attend daily Mass yet feel no desire to go today, and the desolation says, "Do you see who you are? You are a person who does not love the Eucharist." Examples could be multiplied.

In every case, the answer is "No! You are person who loves God, which is why you have a life of prayer, seek closeness with God, and attend daily Mass." You are a person who loves God and whom God is permitting to

[8] *Letters*, 22, emphasis added.

experience spiritual desolation today for reasons of a love that Ignatius will describe later (rule 9). As we have said, if we resist the desolation, we will grow stronger in the spiritual life. If, however, we believe this false equation of spiritual desolation with our spiritual identity, the desolation will weaken us.[9]

Finally, we may consider four qualities, four "voices", of spiritual desolation, all of them lies to be unmasked and rejected.

Shame

A voice says, "Look at you struggling like this! You are such a mess. You should be beyond this after all these years. Shame on you!"

Reply: Again, there is no shame in experiencing spiritual desolation. This is simply what it means to live the spiritual life in a fallen, redeemed, and loved world. Every disciple of Jesus, everyone who has ever loved the Lord, has experienced times of spiritual desolation. What matters is discernment.

Isolation

A voice says, "It's just you. No one else struggles like this. You're the only one."

Reply: Times of spiritual desolation are normal in a well-lived spiritual life. *Everyone* experiences this. Banish this lie of the enemy.

[9] See Timothy M. Gallagher, O.M.V., *Setting Captives Free: Personal Reflections on Ignatian Discernment of Spirits* (Crossroad, 2018), 80–81.

Self-Doubt

A voice says, "Look at you struggling with desolation! There's something wrong with you."

Reply: From all that has been said, the falsity of this lie is evident. There is nothing wrong with you; in fact, there is something very right with you.

A Sense of Irreparable Disaster

A voice says, "It's all over. It's too late. The harm can't be undone."

Reply: Another false assumption of power by the enemy. Spiritual desolation is *never* the end. The enemy is weaker than the good spirit—the infinitely loving God, his angels, his grace—whose light and love always accompany us.

"Pre-Event" Desolation

One common form of spiritual desolation I call "pre-event" desolation. The retreat for which you registered three months ago, the Bible study you usually love, the Saturday afternoon Confession you had planned, the time for today's prayer—these are approaching, and as they do, you find yourself thinking, with a certain heaviness of heart, "Why did I agree to go on the retreat? I won't get much out of it. What's the point of it?" And further: "I don't really want to go to Bible study this evening. Maybe I'll let it go." "I don't feel like going to Confession today; next week will work as well." "I don't really want to pray right now. I can do it later." Of course! There is an enemy who does not want you to do these things, because he knows that if you do, spiritual blessings will follow. When we reject pre-event desolation, we experience post-event consolation.[10]

Witnesses to Rule 4

Saint Charles of Sezze

After beginning his Franciscan novitiate:

Hardly had I put on the habit of St. Francis when such a deep melancholy came over me that my soul was suffocated by an anxiety very difficult for me to describe; difficult, because every part of me was as though abandoned and derelict, without there being a moment of freedom or the least bit of comfort.

I no longer remembered the burning desire and great longing that for such a long time had been mine, to wear the habit of St. Francis; no longer remembered were the many graces our Lord had bestowed on me through the intercession of his most Blessed Mother. How suddenly things had changed! Happiness into bitterness, joy into tears! I was as though beside myself with sadness, buried in a dark night of anxieties, with everything contributing to making my illness even worse. When I looked at the sun its very rays filled me with gloom; the birds with their songs only served to remind me of my affliction; everything I saw or heard made me sad.

That is why I was very much tempted to put off the habit and return to the world! And I believe I would have done so, had the chance been given me and if a special

[10] For a fine literary description of pre-event desolation, read chap. 1 of C. S. Lewis' *Perelandra*.

help of our Lord had been lacking. For two or three weeks I remained in this trouble.[11]

"Deep melancholy", "anxiety", "abandoned", "derelict", "bitterness", "sadness", "gloom", "affliction", "tempted": the trial of spiritual desolation Ignatius describes in rule 4. As Saint Charles notes, temptations mingle with such desolation: "Why continue? Why persevere? Let all this spiritual striving go." Be aware; understand. Name this tactic of the enemy for the discouraging lie that it is, and take action—in this case, rejecting these discouraging lies.

A Parish Priest

On making his morning holy hour:

I feel a heaviness this morning after the difficulties of yesterday, the tiredness, the struggle to find time to pray, up later than usual. I feel the early morning darkness, the cloudy, cold weather, the few people in this big church who have come to pray. The day that lies ahead seems long and lonely. I feel tired, like I won't be able to sustain the work in the parish in these coming weeks, like I'm not doing enough. I don't feel God's closeness, and I feel something sad in me, like I'm far from him. I don't really want to pray this morning, and I feel like nothing will come from this prayer. I feel like all my efforts to pray today will be empty.[12]

A good priest, a man of faithful prayer, whom a loving God permits to experience spiritual desolation for reasons Ignatius will address in rules 7 and 9. Note the degree of awareness in this priest,

[11] *St. Charles of Sezze: Autobiography*, ed. and trans. Leonard Perotti, O.F.M. (Burns & Oates, 1963), 49–50.

[12] Personal testimony shared with permission.

in touch with his spiritual experience, describing it in writing. He exemplifies richly the first step in discernment: Be aware, notice your spiritual experience. He is well on his way to fruitful discernment.

Saint Thérèse of Lisieux

Of the days following her uncle's refusal to allow her to enter Carmel:

Before allowing any ray of hope to shine in my soul, God willed to send me a painful martyrdom lasting *three days*. Oh! never had I understood so well as during this trial, the sorrow of Mary and Joseph during their three-day search for the divine Child Jesus. I was in a sad desert, or rather my soul was like a fragile boat delivered up to the mercy of the waves and having no pilot. I knew Jesus was there sleeping in my boat, but the night was so black it was impossible to see Him; nothing gave me any life, not a single flash came to break the dark clouds.... I felt I was all alone in the garden of Gethsemane like Jesus, and I found no consolation on earth or from heaven; God Himself seemed to have abandoned me.[13]

Intense spiritual desolation of limited duration. The person, Ignatius says, feels "as if separated from one's Creator and Lord". Examples like this indicate why I can say with such surety that there is no shame in experiencing spiritual desolation. Every saint, every man and woman who has ever loved the Lord, has experienced times of spiritual desolation.

[13] *Story of a Soul: The Autobiography of St. Thérèse of Lisieux*, 3rd ed., trans. John Clarke, O.C.D. (ICS Publications, 1996), 109. St. Thérèse also uses the term "dark night" in this quotation. I have discussed the dark night in St. John of the Cross' sense and its relationship to spiritual desolation in *Setting Captives Free*, 71–75. See also Timothy Gallagher, O.M.V., *Struggles in the Spiritual Life: Their Nature and Their Remedies* (Sophia Institute Press, 2022), 157–71.

The Cloud of Unknowing

For the love of God, then, avoid illness as much as possible so that you are not responsible for unnecessary infirmity.

I am serious when I say that this work [the life of prayer] demands a relaxed, healthy, and vigorous disposition of both body and spirit. For the love of God, discipline yourself in body and spirit so that you preserve your health as long as you can. But if, despite your best efforts, illness overtakes you, be patient in bearing it and humbly wait for God's mercy.[14]

Bishop James Conley

I have also found that getting outside into nature is absolutely critical. I have committed myself to two outside walks a day, even if all I have time for is a walk around the block. The fresh air, the beauty of nature, the sun, the wind and the sky all play a part in improving our mood and mental health. An early morning walk as soon as the sun comes up can be very healthy....

[A] podcaster recommended "sun before screens" in the morning. In other words, before you scroll through your phone or get on the computer, go for a walk outside to start your day. Even if it's just a walk around the block, there's something about experiencing nature and being attentive to the beauty around us that is healing for the soul....

A focus on good sleep and healthy eating—which includes drinking enough water—is also a key pillar in supporting mental health. Lastly, I find that enjoying the

[14] *The Cloud of Unknowing and The Book of Privy Counseling*, ed. and trans. William Johnston (Image Books, 1973), 101. The author of this fourteenth-century classic is unknown.

creative works of others is soothing for my soul. Listening to music always lifts me up, and it's amazing what a good novel or a beautiful poem can do when life feels heavy.[15]

Theodore Roosevelt

I have mentioned all these experiences, and I could mention scores of others, because out of them grew my philosophy—perhaps they were in part caused by my philosophy—of bodily vigor as a method of getting that vigor of soul without which vigor of the body counts for nothing.[16]

Notice Roosevelt's principle of "bodily vigor as a method of getting ... vigor of soul". Ignatius supplies a wealth of spiritual tools for rejecting spiritual desolation. As these last quotations attest, however, it is easier to reject desolation if we also make wise use of helpful natural means. When we reduce nonspiritual desolation (tiredness, discouragement), we reduce our vulnerability to spiritual desolation.

Saint Zélie Martin

In a letter to her brother two weeks after the birth of Thérèse:

As for me, I barely sleep more than two hours because I'm almost constantly around the little one, who for some time has been very restless a good part of the night.[17]

[15] Bishop James Conley, "We Are Not Alone. You Are Not Alone!" *Southern Nebraska Register*, May 9, 2025, https://www.lincolndiocese.org/op-ed/bishop-s-column/18800-we-are-not-alone-you-are-not-alone.

[16] *An Autobiography* (Charles Scribner's Sons, 1922), 50.

[17] Blessed Zélie and Louis Martin, *A Call to a Deeper Love: The Family Correspondence of the Parents of St. Thérèse of the Child Jesus (1863–1885)*, trans. Ann Connors Hess, ed. Frances Renda (Society of St. Paul, 2011), 106.

Nonspiritual desolation—in this case, physical tiredness—is holy when embraced out of love for one's vocation, as is evident in Zélie's self-sacrifice for the sake of her newborn child in precarious health. As we have said, after such times, we need healthy ways to restore our energy.

Father Van Exem

In a letter to Archbishop Périer, about Mother Teresa, who shared her recent inspiration to dedicate herself to the poor:

She passed through awful desolation (5 days in May) whilst in Darjeeling and then the idea of the work seemed to be a stupidity (excuse the word, which I think is hers), a treason to her institute and to her superiors; she was in great fear about it all and underwent big temptations. She wrote to me at that time, but I could only pray for her. Happily, the temptation left her after a few days, and again everything is light, joy, trust, and certainty of being on the right path; that is my conviction after seeing her, though I did not talk about her consolations in my interview. When in consolation, she has no doubts at all except at the surface of her soul, she is fearless and ready to immolate everything for Our Lord; in desolation, she did doubt it all, feared a lot, but remained ready to immolate herself.[18]

From Rule 4: "For just as consolation is contrary to desolation [affective level], in the same way the thoughts that come from consolation are contrary to the thoughts that come from desolation [cognitive level]."

[18] *Mother Teresa: Come Be My Light; The Private Writings of the "Saint of Calcutta"*, ed. Brian Kolodiejchuk, M.C. (Image Books, 2007), 72.

Saint Catherine of Siena

I am begging you, since it is so delightful, never let any trouble or temptation the devil might give you make you look back; never let your soul give in to sadness or discouragement, for the devil would like nothing better. He likes to give us lots of annoyances and different sorts of struggles, and suggest false judgments.... He doesn't do this thinking we will fall at the first stroke, but only to lead us to unreasonable sadness and spiritual discouragement. For once he has brought us to sadness and discouragement, we become frustrated with ourselves and abandon our spiritual practices, thinking God must not be pleased or satisfied with what we have been doing, since we are experiencing so much darkness and coldheartedness. We seem to have lost the warmth of clarity, and so we think it better to let go of these practices than to keep them up. Then the devil is happy, because he sees we are ready to be led into despair—and this is the one way he can get us.[19]

"Never let your soul give in to sadness or discouragement." Beginning with rule 5, Ignatius will supply the means to this end.

Venerable Bruno Lanteri

Above all, I beg you with all my might to keep yourself from discouragement, trouble of heart, and sadness, and so, seek constantly to calm your poor heart and encourage it and to serve God always with holy joy; and let your resolutions always be these two, which I counsel you to renew frequently with holy tenacity: first, never to offend

[19] *The Letters of Catherine of Siena*, trans. Suzanne Noffke, O.P., vol. 2 (Arizona Center for Medieval and Renaissance Studies, 2001), 135.

God knowingly, and second, should you commit some failing, never to persevere in this with your will but immediately to lift yourself with humility and courage and to begin again, firmly convinced that God forgives you the moment you ask his forgiveness with humility and trust.[20]

[20] *If You Want Peace in This Life: The Spiritual Letters of Venerable Bruno Lanteri*, trans. Timothy Gallagher, O.M.V. (EWTN Publishing, 2025), 25. For complementary quotations, see Timothy M. Gallagher, O.M.V., *The Discernment of Spirits: An Ignatian Guide for Everyday Living* (Crossroad, 2005): Blessed Stefan Cardinal Wyszynski (68), St. Teresa of Calcutta (73).

Rule 5

Make No Change in Desolation

Ignatius' classic rule 5 reads as follows:

> **Fifth Rule.** In time of desolation never make a change, but be firm and constant in the proposals and determination in which one was the day preceding such desolation, or in the determination in which one was in the preceding consolation. Because, as in consolation the good spirit guides and counsels us more, so in desolation the bad spirit, with whose counsels we cannot find the way to a right decision.

Eight succinct and magisterial words: "In time of desolation never make a change." That is, in time of spiritual desolation, never make a change to any spiritual proposal you had in place before that desolation began. On the contrary, remain *firm* (unyielding) and *constant* (unyielding through the time of desolation) in the spiritual proposals you chose before the desolation began.

A man registers for an online course on prayer. A woman plans to go to Confession at 4:00 P.M. on Saturday. A man prays Evening Prayer from the Liturgy of the Hours when he returns from work. A woman goes to daily Mass when her occupations permit. All of them, in time of spiritual desolation, when God feels distant and energy for spiritual things wanes, consider changing their spiritual proposals: the man, withdrawing from the online course; the woman, omitting Confession on Saturday; the other man, neglecting Evening Prayer; the other woman, missing daily Mass when she could go.

In every case, Ignatius' rule 5 provides the clarity they need. Two questions suffice:

1. Am I in a time of spiritual desolation?
2. Am I, in a time of spiritual desolation, considering changing a spiritual proposal that I had in place before the desolation began?

Whenever the answer to both questions is yes, these persons know with absolute clarity ("never", the rule says) that they should *not* make those changes but should remain firm and constant in what they had planned before the desolation began. Of course the enemy wants them to change their proposals! If they do not make the suggested changes but remain firm in their proposals, very likely that online course, Confession, Evening Prayer, and Mass will weaken the desolation or eliminate it altogether. If they do make these changes, the desolation will persist and is likely to increase.

Such is the norm. The reason for the norm follows: In the experience envisaged in these fourteen rules, the good spirit guides and counsels us in spiritual consolation; in spiritual desolation, the enemy, "with whose counsels we cannot find the way to a right decision".

Rule 5, faithfully observed, will guide us safely through almost any darkness in the spiritual life. It will save us from harmful decisions and keep us solidly on the path God desires. For many years, I have seen this rule save vocations, marriages, programs of spiritual studies, times of prayer, and many other "proposals" in the spiritual life.

Rule 5 does not say that we may never make changes in our spiritual proposals. It says that we should never make such changes *when we are in spiritual desolation.*

We are not, however, always in spiritual desolation. In time of spiritual consolation or in the serenity of what Ignatius calls "the tranquil time",[1] beneficial changes may be explored: new steps in prayer, greater closeness to the Eucharist, growth in one's vocation, and similar endeavors. Should the changes under consideration be significant, conversation with a wise and competent spiritual person would be valuable.

When consolation or a tranquil time returns after desolation, we will perceive that those changes, which in desolation seemed so clear, necessary, and urgent, are not at all necessary and would in fact be harmful. One spiritual director sums up rule 5 by saying, "What you decide in the light, do not change in the darkness." This rule is a friend for the entire spiritual journey.

The Life-Changing Power of Rule 5

I beg of you: Never forget rule 5. As said, it will get you safely through almost any spiritual darkness you may ever experience.

I invite you to say these eight key words out loud: "In time of desolation, never make a change." Say them a second time.

I had just finished speaking about rule 5 to a parish group. In the break before the next talk, a woman approached me. She had been present twenty years earlier

[1] *SpirEx* 177.

when I taught these rules. She told me that in a time of deep darkness, rule 5 had saved her life. The next person in line heard what she said. When she, too, approached, she said quietly, "Rule 5 saved my marriage." One day, this simple rule might save you too.

Witnesses to Rule 5

Saint Ignatius of Loyola

It is an attribute of God our Lord to be unchangeable, and a quality of the enemy to be inconstant and changeable.[2]

Archbishop François Fénelon

I am sure that you can see how dangerous it is to make decisions when we are in the agonies of distress and under the influence of violent temptations. This is one sure way to go astray. You may ask any experienced [director] you wish, and I am sure he will tell you that you should not make any decisions until you have quieted down. And he will tell you that the easiest way to deceive yourself is to trust your hours of decision making in a time of suffering. At such a time as this, your mind is too unsettled to be trusted.... So I strongly advise you to wait until you are in a better condition to accept counsel from the Lord.[3]

[2] *The Spiritual Diary of St. Ignatius Loyola: Text and Commentary*, trans. Simon Decloux, S.J. (Centrum Ignatianum Spiritualitatis, 1990), 81.

[3] *Let Go* (Whitaker House, 1973), 55. The text uses the word "counselor"; I have changed this to "director" to avoid confusion between spiritual direction and psychological counseling.

Blessed James Alberione

Spiritual desolation is an obscuring of the spirit, a disturbance, a strong enticement toward low and earthly things.... It is a rule of the saints that no resolution is to be abandoned during these trying moments, and no practice is to be omitted; one should carry out all his previous resolutions with constancy. It is precisely at such a time that prayer, meditation, examination of conscience and mortification of the senses must be intensified.[4]

Jules Toner, S.J.

One last comment on [rule 5]: the importance of this rule and the need for calling it to attention can hardly be overestimated. To forget it in lesser matters, or to fail to follow it when it is remembered, can lead to entanglements and vexations that impede personal growth in Christian life, and also to waste of time and energy on projects that are irrelevant to God's work in the world or even a hindrance to it. To forget the rule in greater matters can lead to great harm. Yet in time of desolation we so easily forget the guiding principle put down in this rule. Even those who know it well do this. It would be conservative to say that nine out of ten times any suggested change of decision about our spiritual life or apostolate which we thought of during spiritual desolation seems undesirable or even foolish when the desolation has passed; and that ten out of ten times we will be glad that we waited and do not have

[4] *The Paschal Mystery and Christian Living* (Pauline Books & Media, 1968), 54, 57. Blessed Alberione links rules 5 and 6 in this quote.

to live with consequences of a decision made in circumstances which call that decision into question.[5]

A Woman

My son died in a tragic way. It was terribly hard. I had been exposed to Saint Ignatius' rules, and I remembered rule 5. Not long before, I had begun to pray daily with Scripture. I knew that rule 5 told me that I should not let this go in the darkness I felt. I wasn't able to absorb the same amount of Scripture, but I kept at it faithfully. It got me through this. Praying this way, I felt a certain joy even in my sorrow.[6]

[5] *A Commentary on Saint Ignatius' Rules for the Discernment of Spirits: A Guide to the Principles and Practice* (Institute of Jesuit Sources, 1982), 155.

[6] Paraphrased from an interview on Relevant Radio, 2025. For complementary quotations, see Timothy M. Gallagher, O.M.V., *The Discernment of Spirits: An Ignatian Guide for Everyday Living* (Crossroad, 2005): St. Ignatius (80–83).

Rule 6

Resist Desolation with Good Actions

Saint Ignatius pairs rule 6 with rule 5 as its necessary complement. In rule 5, he describes the changes we should *not* make in desolation; in rule 6, he identifies those of a different kind that we *should* make.

He writes:

> Sixth Rule. Although in desolation we should not change our first proposals, it is very advantageous to change ourselves intensely against the desolation itself, as by insisting more upon prayer, meditation, upon much examination, and upon extending ourselves in some suitable way of doing penance.

"Although in desolation we should not change our first proposals": Saint Ignatius' opening words summarize rule 5 and explicitly link it with rule 6. Rule 5: In desolation, we should not change our spiritual proposals. Rule 6: It is very advantageous to change *ourselves*, "intensely"—that is, with energy—"against the desolation itself", using the spiritual means provided in these rules.

A crucial point for the spiritual life is touched upon here: God *never* asks us to bear spiritual desolation passively. The call is always actively to reject these discouraging lies of the enemy—to change ourselves intensely against the desolation. This, Ignatius tells us, will be not only advantageous but *very* advantageous in the spiritual life. The difference between unhappily enduring spiritual desolation until it eventually passes (who can say how long this may be?) and actively changing ourselves intensely against it, using the spiritual means Ignatius outlines, is enormous and liberating. That difference is the heart of rule 6.

Some difficulties God does ask us to bear: burdens of poor health, the weight of our responsibilities, and the like. This is the cross that Jesus told us would be a daily part of discipleship (Lk 9:23). He also promised that when we carry our crosses, faithfully following him, our Good Fridays, like his, will lead to Easter Sundays of new life in us and, through us, in others. But we are *never* asked to bear passively the discouraging lies of spiritual desolation. Here, the call is always actively to employ the means to reject it.[1]

In rule 6, Ignatius proposes four such spiritual means: prayer, meditation, much examination, and some suitable way of doing penance. Obviously, these are spiritually beneficial practices in general. In rule 6, however, Ignatius speaks to those of us struggling with spiritual desolation *right now* and counsels us to apply these means in a specific way, one that will help us reject the desolation. We do this, he writes, by "insisting more" upon these in our battle with desolation and by "extending ourselves" in a precise way of applying them. We will look at each from this perspective.

[1] The same is not true of the dark night in St. John of the Cross' sense; this is a work of God. On the difference between spiritual desolation and the dark night, see the references given in note 13 in the chapter on rule 4.

Prayer

This is, most basically, prayer of petition. The first means Ignatius offers to one struggling with spiritual desolation is to *ask for help*. This can be very simple: "Father, be with me. Jesus, I need your help. Holy Spirit, strengthen me. Mary, be my Mother. My angel, guide me. Saint ______, pray for me."

We have a promise: "Ask and it will be given to you" (Mt 7:7, NABRE) and "Whatever you ask in my name, I will do" (Jn 14:13, NABRE). Experience teaches us the power of such petitionary prayer when we make it in time of desolation. I believe that not by accident Ignatius placed this "means" first: humbly, sincerely, from our need, and aware of our weakness, to ask for the divine love and power that can set us free.

Meditation

Again, this counsel is directed to the one struggling with spiritual desolation. Ignatius calls this person to a meditation directed specifically against the desolation, as a help to overcome it. I offer here some concrete suggestions regarding forms this meditation might take.

Truths of Faith

A man sits at his desk at the end of a discouraging day with no feeling of God's closeness and no desire for his customary prayer at this time. He pauses, and he consciously reflects on God's loving providence in his life, on God's love for him, on Jesus' saving power and grace, and on Mary's love and closeness. For a few minutes, he focuses his mind and heart on these truths. Now he is more prepared to pray.

Verses of Scripture

A woman arose this morning feeling desolate, far from God, with no energy for spiritual things, inclined to indulge in social media. She takes her Bible in hand and slowly reads verses that speak to her of God's faithful, protecting love: "The LORD is my shepherd; there is nothing I lack. . . . Even though I walk through the valley of the shadow of death, I will fear no evil, for you are with me" (Ps 23:1, 4, NABRE); "I can do all things in him who strengthens me" (Phil 4:13); "The LORD is my light and my salvation; whom should I fear?" (Ps 27:1, NABRE). As she slowly reads these verses, the heaviness begins to lift.

A recommendation: Know the biblical verses that speak to you of God's faithful love. Have them ready so you can call them to mind—meditate on them—in time of desolation.

Memories of God's Fidelity in the Past

In the present struggle with spiritual desolation, recall how God has always brought you safely through such times in the past. Reflect on these past times, meditate on them, and you will find greater courage to resist desolation in the present.

An Anti-Desolation Song

"With the harp I will solve my problem" (Ps 49:4).[2] Is there a hymn or song that encourages you in times of spiritual darkness? If you play an instrument, play and sing that hymn or song. Or go online, sing it as you listen, reflect (meditate) on its message, and allow the Lord to lift your heart through it. The beauty of melody with words can be a rich form of meditation against the weight of desolation.

Something for the Eye to See

Similar to the preceding paragraph, this counsel invites us to enlist the body in our response to spiritual desolation. We are not pure spirits; we are incarnate spirits. The more of our humanity we engage in the battle against spiritual desolation, the more effective our response will be. Concretely, if you have a journal and have recorded past struggles with desolation and how, with God's help, you overcame them, open it and reread what you wrote then. Consider placing images of Jesus, Mary, the angels, or your favorite saints where you will see them in the time of conflict—the sight of them will lead you more easily to prayer. Keep a Bible close at hand and read from it.

A Suggestion: Spiritual Arrows

Fill your spiritual quiver with spiritual arrows to launch against spiritual desolation. Have these ready before the

[2] *The Liturgy of the Hours*, vol. 2 (Catholic Book Publishing, 1976), 1273.

desolation begins. If you do, they will be more readily available when desolation does return. Spiritual arrows include truths of faith, Bible verses, memories of God's fidelity, your anti-desolation song, and the images in your home or on your desk at work. One person shared with me his anti-desolation card—Bible verses, prayers, sayings of the saints—to which he turns in time of spiritual desolation. A great initiative, worthy of imitation.

Much Examination

As we have said, the unexamined, unaware, undiscerning response to spiritual desolation is flight into what appears more gratifying, into what Blaise Pascal calls "diversion": refrigerators, YouTube, Netflix, social media, television, movies, computer games, gossip. When we put down the phone, turn off the television, and close the refrigerator for the last time, the desolation remains, most likely heavier as a result of the diversion.

Instead of this, Ignatius asks us to stand our ground and *examine what we are experiencing*. Two questions are especially helpful in this examination:

1. "What am I feeling?"
2. "How did this begin?"

"What am I feeling?" Simply to name the experience as spiritual desolation is enormously liberating. Knowing it to be spiritual desolation, we know how to respond. The answer to this question brings us to the second step in discernment (be aware, *understand*) and prepares the way for the third (*take action*—in this case, reject).

"How did this begin?" What appears as global, overwhelming spiritual desolation is very difficult to resist. It is much easier to resist if we can identify when it began:

- "When I had that difficult conversation with that person"
- "When that project at work did not go well"
- "When I made this effort and did not succeed"
- "When I heard that news"
- "When I received that email"
- "When I read that text"

In each case, we can plan helpful steps to respond to the difficulty. When we pinpoint how the desolation began and plan a helpful response, much of its burden is lifted.

The passage from "myself-in-desolation", submerged in it and fleeing from it into diversion, to "myself-reflecting-on-myself-in-desolation",[3] able to name it and choose steps to overcome it, is powerful. Ignatius warmly encourages this passage; he counsels *much* examination.

This is not a cold exercise of introspection. The examination is prayer. We do this in relationship with the Father, whose beloved sons and daughters we are; with Jesus our Savior; with the Holy Spirit, who is Light and Love; with Mary, our Mother in the order of grace. We do this as part of the communion of saints.

Two further spiritual means assist this examination: the daily examen prayer[4] and, where possible, conversation with

[3] Jules Toner, S.J., *A Commentary on Saint Ignatius' Rules for the Discernment of Spirits: A Guide to the Principles and Practice* (Institute of Jesuit Sources, 1982), 151.

[4] Timothy M. Gallagher, O.M.V., *The Examen Prayer: Ignatian Wisdom for Our Lives Today* (Crossroad, 2006). See also the Discerning Hearts app and Timothy Gallagher, O.M.V., "What Is an Examen", YouTube video, 27:22, https://www.youtube.com/watch?v=qD1Bs6l-agw.

a wise and competent spiritual guide. Ignatius will discuss such conversation in rule 13.

Suitable Penance

Instead of our fleeing into diversion that only prolongs the desolation, Ignatius calls us to *suitable gestures of penitential courage*. No matter how small, these have great power to weaken and banish desolation. Ignatius speaks of "suitable" penance—that is, penance well directed against the discouraging lies of the desolation.

These penances may be quite small. Wait ten minutes before going to the refrigerator. God can do much in ten minutes! Wait ten—even five—minutes before going online again. God can do much in five minutes. Smile at that person when it is the last thing you want to do. Perform a small service for someone: Answer that email from the person waiting for a reply or return that borrowed item. Go for a walk, do ten minutes of exercise, or make a similar gesture of penitential courage.

These small steps strengthen us, and they prepare us to take further steps. Such acts of penitential courage counter the tendency to flee into diversion and greatly strengthen us against desolation.

Saint Thérèse of Lisieux says, "God never refuses that first grace that gives one the courage to act; afterwards, the heart is strengthened, and one advances from victory to victory."[5] This is precisely Ignatius' counsel.

What will happen if, in time of spiritual desolation, we turn to God with prayer of petition, meditate on truths

[5] *St. Thérèse of Lisieux: Her Last Conversations*, trans. John Clarke, O.C.D. (ICS Publications, 1977), 142.

that assure us of God's faithful love and power, examine what we are experiencing, and make suitable gestures of penitential courage? What will *not* happen is intense and prolonged desolation. The struggle may not pass immediately, but it will be much lighter and end much sooner—a wonderful change of spiritual space.

Leave Your Room

Classically, it was said, "Stay in your cell [i.e., your room], and your cell will teach you everything."[6] I believe that with the advent of the digital world, the contrary is often true. Sometimes, perhaps often, the best thing you can do when in desolation is to leave your room. There, it is so easy to escape into the digital realm, and this never solves desolation. Leave the room: You will meet someone, you can attend to a task, you can pray, you can exercise, you can refill your water bottle ... When you return to your room, the darkness will no longer be so dark.

I find that exercise is often the way out of desolation. You feel exhausted, worn out. When you exercise, even if only lightly, you begin to feel better. "But I don't have the energy to exercise for forty-five minutes!" Perhaps not, but can you exercise for ten? Saint Pierre Favre says, "Attend to the smallest things, examine them, think about putting them into effect, and the Lord will grant you greater."[7]

[6] Attributed to Saint Moses the Black, *The Sayings of the Desert Fathers: The Alphabetical Collection*, trans. Benedicta Ward, S.L.G. (Cistercian Publications, 1975), 118.

[7] Saint Pierre Favre, quoted in Jim Manney, *An Ignatian Book of Days: Daily Reflections from the Spiritual Wisdom of St. Ignatius of Loyola* (Loyola Press, 2014), 24.

Spiritual Arrows

After we went through rule 6, a young man said the following: "When things were not going well, I thought all I could say was 'I'm having a bad day.' Now I find that I can examine what is happening, name what is going on, and see the way to reject the darkness." On another occasion, a woman told me, "I came from a tough meeting, and I was hurt. I needed to take time after the meeting to understand it all. I find that if I can make sense of things and come to understand them, I can handle almost anything." She is right. This is why Ignatius calls us to "much examination" in time of spiritual desolation.

In her final months of physical and spiritual struggle, Saint Thérèse of Lisieux kept before her eyes the statue of Mary that she loved, and she pinned to the curtain of her bed a picture of Blessed Théophane Vénard, whose cause of canonization had been recently introduced; photos of her brothers and sisters who died young and to whose intercession she turned for help; and small images of Our Lady of Sorrows, Saint Joseph with the Child Jesus, Saint Cecilia, and the *Ecce Homo* (Christ crowned with thorns).[8] These were wise choices in a time of struggle and a pattern to be imitated, by each of us in our own way.

After I presented these Ignatian rules to the priests in a certain diocese, they prepared a short anti-desolation card for all the priests of the diocese. This was a bifold card with biblical verses, writings from saints, and short prayers—"spiritual arrows" they could have at

[8] Helmuth Nils Loose and Pierre Descouvemont, *Thérèse et Lisieux* (Editions du Cerf, 1991), 294, 297.

hand in time of spiritual desolation. Another wonderful choice.

Witnesses to Rule 6

Saint Alphonsus Liguori

I repeat, the most effective and most necessary of all remedies against temptations, the remedy of remedies, is to pray to God for help and to continue praying as long as the temptation lasts. Often the Lord will have decreed that victory will come, not at the first prayer, but at the second, third, or fourth. In short, we must persuade ourselves that all our welfare depends on prayer; changing our lives depends on prayer, conquering temptations depends on prayer; obtaining divine love—along with perfection, perseverance, and eternal salvation—depends upon prayer.[9]

Saint Thérèse of Lisieux

At each new occasion of combat, when my enemies provoke me, I conduct myself bravely. Knowing that it is cowardly to enter into a duel, I turn my back on my adversaries without even looking them in the face, but I run toward Jesus.[10]

"I run toward Jesus": a lovely metaphor for the prayer of petition Ignatius counsels in time of spiritual desolation.

[9] *The Practice of the Love of Jesus Christ* (Liguori Publications, 1999), 193–94.

[10] *Oeuvres Complètes* (Éditions du Cerf, Desclée de Brouwer, 1996), 243, author's translation, with slight variations on that of *Story of a Soul: The Autobiography of St. Thérèse of Lisieux*, 3rd ed., trans. John Clarke, O.C.D. (ICS Publications, 1996), 213.

Flannery O'Connor

The only force I believe in is prayer, and it is a force I apply with more doggedness than attention.[11]

Saint Teresa of Avila

I don't understand these fears, "The devil! The devil!", when we can say "God! God!", and make the devil tremble.[12]

Pope Benedict XVI

In the words of Saint Bernard, I invite everyone to become a trusting child before Mary, even as the Son of God did. Saint Bernard says, and we say with him: "Look to the star of the sea, call upon Mary ... in danger, in distress, in doubt, think of Mary, call upon Mary. May her name never be far from your lips, or far from your heart ... If you follow her, you will not stray; if you pray to her, you will not despair; if you turn your thoughts to her, you will not err. If she holds you, you will not fall; if she protects you, you need not fear; if she is your guide, you will not tire; if she is gracious to you, you will surely reach your destination."[13]

In time of spiritual desolation, "Think of Mary, call upon Mary." "If she holds you, you will not fall." After the Lord himself,

[11] *Flannery O'Connor: The Habit of Being*, ed. Sally Fitzgerald (Farrar, Straus and Giroux, 1979), 100.

[12] *The Book of Her Life*, in *The Collected Works of St. Teresa of Avila*, trans. Kieran Kavanaugh, O.C.D., and Otilio Rodriguez, O.C.D., vol. 1 (ICS Publications, 1976), 170.

[13] Address at Heiligenkreuz Abbey (Austria, September 9, 2007), https://www.vatican.va/content/benedict-xvi/en/speeches/2007/september/documents/hf_ben-xvi_spe_20070909_heiligenkreuz.html#_ftnref4, ellipses in original.

Mary is our greatest defender in time of desolation. "Never was it known that anyone who fled to thy protection, implored thy help, or sought thy intercession was left unaided" (the Memorare). Never. Turn to Mary in time of spiritual desolation. You will always find help there.

Saint Theodoros the Great Ascetic (Orthodox)

One of the ancients spoke wisely and simply about thoughts. Judge thoughts, he said, before the judgment seat of the heart, to discern whether they are ours or those of our enemy. Place those which are good and properly our own in the inmost shrine of the soul, keeping them in this inviolable treasury. But chastise hostile thoughts with the whip of the intelligence and banish them, giving them no place, no abode within the bounds of your soul. Or, to speak more fittingly, slay them completely with the sword of prayer and divine meditation, so that when the robbers have been destroyed, their chief may take fright. For, so he says, a man who examines his thoughts strictly is one who also truly loves the commandments.[14]

"Chastise hostile thoughts.... Slay them completely with the sword of prayer and divine meditation." In time of spiritual desolation, extend yourself, Ignatius says, in prayer and meditation.

Julien Green (Novelist)

The Bible has been a spring where I have drunk freely in times of distress and on the banks of these living waters

[14] "Theodoros the Great Ascetic: A Century of Spiritual Texts", https://orthodoxchurchfathers.com/fathers/philokalia/theodoros-the-great-ascetic-a-century-of-spiritual-texts.html.

have lain me down to dream of splendid *elsewheres*, from which all pain has been driven away.[15]

Evagrius of Pontus

In a rich example of scriptural meditation against desolation, Evagrius gives 498 biblical passages for meditation in times of various struggles with the enemy, with these among them:

Against the soul that, in the time of sadness, wants to find in prayer spiritual words: "Do not forsake me, Lord; my God, do not depart from me. Come near to help me, Lord of my salvation" (Ps 37:22–23).

Against the thought that prophesies to me severe sufferings that come from temptations: "I consider that the sufferings of the present time are not worth comparing with the glory about to be revealed to us" (Rom 8:18).

Against the demon that brings to me the sins of my youth: "Everything old has passed away; see, everything has become new" (2 Cor 5:17).

To the Lord concerning the thoughts of listlessness that persist in me: "Look upon my affliction and my trouble, and forgive all my sins" (Ps 24:18).

Against the thoughts of listlessness that take away my hope: "I believe that I will see the good things of the Lord in the land of the living" (Ps 26:13).

[15] *Diary, 1928–1957*, ed. Kurt Wolff, trans. Anne Green (Harcourt, Brace & World, 1964), 105.

Against the thought of listlessness that takes away the hope of our endurance on the pretext that one cannot through its duration persuade the Lord to have mercy on us: "I waited patiently for the Lord and he attended to me and listened to my supplication" (Ps 39:2).[16]

Pope Saint John Paul II

It is pleasant to spend time with him, to lie close to his breast like the Beloved Disciple (cf. Jn 13:25) and to feel the infinite love present in his heart. If in our time Christians must be distinguished above all by the "art of prayer," how can we not feel a renewed need to spend time in spiritual converse, in silent adoration, in heartfelt love before Christ present in the Most Holy Sacrament? How often, dear brother and sisters, have I experienced this, and drawn from it strength, consolation and support![17]

Blessed Solanus Casey

The answer to all problems is Mass and Holy Communion.[18]

[16] *Talking Back: A Monastic Handbook for Combating Demons*, trans. David Brakke (Liturgical Press, 2009), 108, 116, 136, 137.

[17] Encyclical letter *Ecclesia de Eucharistia* (April 17, 2003), no. 25, https://www.vatican.va/content/john-paul-ii/en/encyclicals/documents/hf_jp-ii_enc_20030417_eccl-de-euch.html.

[18] *Blessed Solanus Casey: The Official Account of a Virtuous Life*, ed. Michael Crosby, O.F.M. Cap. (Crossroad, 2002), 182.

Raïssa Maritain

Religious music in some way unties the knot between body and spirit. It frees the soul, exalts it toward a more spiritual life.[19]

Religious music can be a great help in the struggle against spiritual desolation.

Saint John Vianney

Man, who is a creature composed of a body and a soul, requires perceptible objects to represent to him the unseen, or, in other words, he needs sacred pictures. From the visible our human thoughts rise up to the invisible; by that which is visible we are reminded of that which is invisible; by the natural of the supernatural. That is why, from the very earliest ages, Christians made pictures of the Divine Savior, of the Mother of God, and of the angels.[20]

Saint John of the Cross

Frequent combing gives the hair more luster and makes it easier to comb; a soul that frequently examines its thoughts, words, and deeds, which are its hair, doing all things for the love of God, will have lustrous hair. Then the Bridegroom will look on the neck of the bride and thereby be captivated; and will be wounded by one of her

[19] *Raïssa's Journal*, ed. Jacques Maritain (Magi, 1974), 164.

[20] *Sermons for the Sundays and Feasts of the Year by the Ven. Curé of Ars* (Neumann Press, 1984), 77.

eyes, that is, by the purity of intention she has in all she does [Song 4:9].[21]

"A soul that frequently examines its thoughts, words, and deeds". Saint Ignatius: "much examination".

Servant of God Dorothy Day

Peggy Conklin [a woman who was ill] too, enjoying each day—her flowers, her cats, her books, the company that drops in to see her.

To list them all. In keeping a notebook it is good to look back on in moments of suffering when the Cross seems unendurable.[22]

I awake in the morning with all the problems around me pressing me down. Always in my life I have found that with writing about them, putting them down on paper, I can lift the burden from my heart.[23]

I find the same. When I am in desolation and cannot seem to find freedom from it, I take my journal and write out what I am feeling and, as much as I can see of this, its cause as well. Invariably, this lightens my heart and sometimes breaks the hold of the desolation. I see more clearly what is happening and what I need to do about it.

A beautiful sunrise. Gulls on the big rock offshore. Low tide, sometimes one wakes depressed in September. Problems on

[21] *The Sayings of Light and Love*, in *The Collected Works of St. John of the Cross*, 3rd ed., trans. Kieran Kavanaugh, O.C.D., and Otilio Rodriguez, O.C.D. (ICS Publications, 1991), 93.

[22] *The Duty of Delight: The Diaries of Dorothy Day*, ed. Robert Ellsberg (Marquette University Press, 2008), 462.

[23] *The Duty of Delight*, 491.

every side. One cannot help but share them. The Human condition. Saint Paul writes, "Rejoice! Again I say rejoice." Work. Clean a room, a desk, clean oneself up![24]

Sometimes there is nothing on this earth we want, and I've been through those times. Neither food nor drink, not a movie or downtown or a new hat, not a book or anything else. Father Farina calls them tunnels and temptation to discouragement. I always get through them by manual work. Or take a walk.[25]

In time of desolation, this kind of "penance" may well free us from the darkness: Work. Clean a room. Put order into one's things and one's self. Do manual work. Take a walk.

Saint Pierre Favre

Seek grace for the smallest things, and you will also find grace to accomplish, to believe in, and to hope for the greatest things. Attend to the smallest things, examine them, think about putting them into effect, and the Lord will grant you greater. Extend yourself, and give yourself up fully to doing what you can with a little grace from God, and the Lord will grant you a great grace that will enable you to perform even what is beyond your capabilities.[26]

This is the dynamic of the suitable penance Ignatius counsels. Even small steps to resist the desolation have great power to prepare the next step, and the next. Yes, "seek grace for the smallest things" and take these small steps.

[24] *The Duty of Delight*, 587.

[25] Quoted in Kate Hennessy, *Dorothy Day: The World Will Be Saved by Beauty: An Intimate Portrait of My Grandmother* (Scribner, 2017), 192.

[26] *The Spiritual Writings of Pierre Favre*, trans. Edmond Murphy, S.J., and Martin Palmer, S.J. (Institute of Jesuit Sources, 1996), 159.

Rule 7

Resist Desolation with Good Thoughts

In rule 7, Ignatius offers further help for the person battling with spiritual desolation. He turns now to a set of interrelated *thoughts* that will fortify the person in this struggle:

> Seventh Rule. Let one who is in desolation consider how the Lord has left him in trial in his natural powers so that he may resist the various agitations and temptations of the enemy; because he can resist with the divine help, which always remains with him, though he does not clearly feel it; for the Lord has taken away from him his great fervor, abundant love, and intense grace, leaving him, however, sufficient grace for eternal salvation.

The key word in rule 7 is *consider*: "Let one who is in desolation consider"—that is, call to mind, think about, reflect on, and ponder—these three interrelated thoughts:

1. This spiritual desolation is a trial—that is, it lies within God's providence.
2. The purpose of the trial is to permit resistance to spiritual desolation and, through resistance, to enable growth in the ability to resist.
3. The individual can resist the desolation because God always gives the necessary grace for this resistance.

A Trial

"Let one who is in desolation consider how *the Lord* has left him in trial in his natural powers." A man sits at his desk at 10:00 P.M., feeling discouraged, far from God, with no desire to pray as he normally does; a woman sits in the kitchen at 4:00 P.M., disheartened after a difficult day of teaching, with no energy for prayer, no feeling of God's love, inclined to call a friend for a conversation that she knows will descend into gossip. Let them *consider* that this is not empty pain, blind fate, or useless suffering but that this is a *trial the Lord is calling them to endure* (Acts 14:22). Let them consider, the man at his desk and the woman in the kitchen, that this experience is within God's loving providence, that it *has meaning*.

Meaningless pain is difficult to sustain, and we are likely to succumb to it. If the man and the woman view their spiritual desolation in this way, they may well surrender to it. If, however, they *consider* that this desolation is permitted *by God* as a trial—the reason for which Ignatius will describe immediately—they will be greatly fortified to overcome it.

The Purpose of the Trial

Further, let this person reflect on the *reason* why God is permitting the trial: "so that he may resist the various agitations and temptations of the enemy". We grow in patience by undergoing situations that require the exercise of patience. We grow in prayer by exercising the act of prayer. We grow in Christ-centered love of difficult persons by spending time with them and exercising Christ-centered love of neighbor.

We grow in a virtue precisely by exercising the act of that virtue. Likewise, we grow in the ability to resist spiritual desolation by experiencing such desolation and actively resisting it. If it is true, as we have said, that for most of us spiritual desolation—when we grow discouraged and are inclined to regress—is our main obstacle, then the ability to resist it is one of the greatest gifts God can give us.

Each time we resist spiritual desolation, two things happen: We avoid harm from that desolation, and we grow in the ability to resist future desolation. When, Ignatius says, people experience spiritual desolation, let them consider God's purpose in allowing this trial. If they do, their energy to resist it will increase.

"I Can't" and "I Can"

The litany of spiritual desolation is this: "I can't, I can't, I can't ..." "I can't pray today." "I can't finish this time of prayer." "I can't go to the Bible study." "I can't go to daily Mass as I usually do." "I can't go on that retreat." "I can't continue these efforts to grow spiritually." In this case, the "I can't" arises not from occupations, issues of health, or similar valid reasons but rather from the discouragement of the spiritual desolation itself.

When desolation cries out "You can't!" consider, Ignatius says, the truth that *you can*: You can pray, can finish the time of prayer, can go to the Bible study, can go to Mass, can go on retreat. Why can you do these things? Ignatius answers, "He can resist with the divine help, which always remains with him, though he does not clearly feel it." Yes, the Lord "has taken away from him his great fervor, abundant love, and intense grace"—that is, the joy of spiritual consolation—and so he cannot *feel* this divine help. Let him, however, *consider* that such divine help is always present. He has "sufficient grace", all the grace he needs, to resist the spiritual desolation and remain solidly on track toward eternal salvation. This divine help, Ignatius affirms, is *always* given to us in time of desolation.

Spiritual desolation, dark though it may be, can never touch a deeper grace that God always gives: a divine help, a sufficient grace, all the spiritual strength we need to overcome the desolation. Consider this truth, Ignatius says, in time of desolation.

If the man at 10:00 P.M. and the woman at 4:00 P.M. *do not* consider this truth, they are likely to yield to the desolation and turn to diversion. If they *do* consider this truth and understand with certitude that they *can* resist the desolation, they are much more likely to resist it. Such is the wisdom of rule 7.

God Uses Our Desolation

My heart lifts when people grasp the truth of rule 7. They tend to say something like this: "When 'failures' became 'trials', everything changed. Struggles used to mean to me that I was a failure. Now they are trials to be borne with trust in God. And I see the fruitfulness of these trials in my life."

A retreatant prays four times in the course of the retreat day. Two of the prayer periods are filled with spiritual consolation, two with spiritual desolation. He says, "Well, at least two of the prayer times were fruitful." No. All four lay within a divine providence that gave joy and energy through spiritual consolation, while permitting the trial of spiritual desolation, so that, by resisting, the retreatant would grow in other important ways. God's love was at work in all four prayer times. The same is true in our daily lives both in times of spiritual consolation and in times of spiritual desolation.

Witnesses to Rule 7

Saint Philip Neri

The way that God takes with the souls that love him, by allowing them to be tempted and to fall into tribulations, is a true espousal between himself and them.[1]

God allows temptations and tribulations as a true espousal of the soul with himself. A beautiful way to "consider that the Lord has left him in trial in his natural powers": an espousal.

A Letter Written by the Author of The Cloud of Unknowing

No one knows the hidden dispositions of a man except that inward spirit of the man himself. It is possible that you do not know your own inward dispositions as fully as you will later on, when God makes you aware of them through the bitter experience of frequent failure and new beginnings. For I never knew any sinner come to the perfect knowledge of himself and his own inward dispositions, unless he learned it in God's school, by experiencing many temptations.[2]

[1] *The Maxims and Sayings of St. Philip Neri*, trans. F. W. Faber (St. Athanasius Press, 2009), September 25, Kindle, loc. 350.

[2] "Letter on Discerning Spiritual Impulses", *The Way*, no. 1 (1961): 226.

Dr. Kevin Majeres (Catholic Psychiatrist)

It is the challenge we are avoiding that actually contains the deepest growth we need, and that will make us the happiest.... When we are helping people reframe a challenge that right now they are facing and that they might see as a threat, what we want to do is help them see it as an opportunity for some kind of learning, growth, or practice, asking the question: How can this bring out the best in me right now? ... Asking this question is like asking: In what way is this the perfect challenge for me right now? ...

What this is also getting at is, is there a providence behind every challenge? Can this challenge have a new light through the operation of faith in my mind? ... In any single challenge, faith actually can show you how this makes sense as the will of God for your sanctification.[3]

"Can this challenge have a new light through the operation of faith in my mind?" In regard to spiritual desolation, Ignatius answered this question five hundred years ago: The call, right now, to resist spiritual desolation is a trial. It lies within God's loving providence precisely as an opportunity for spiritual growth. To consider this in time of spiritual desolation is enormously strengthening.

Venerable Bruno Lanteri

All that will happen to me, whether favorable or unfavorable, is prepared for me by God as an occasion of gain, may he ever be praised; I desire to profit from it.[4]

[3] John Heinen and Sam Guzman, hosts, *The Catholic Gentleman*, podcast, episode 52, "Embracing the Cross and Overcoming Anxiety", March 16, 2022, https://catholicgentleman.com/2022/03/embracing-the-cross-and-overcoming-anxiety/.

[4] Timothy Gallagher, O.M.V., *Begin Again: The Life and Spiritual Legacy of Bruno Lanteri* (Crossroad, 2013), 147.

You tell me that you are troubled by temptations. Take care, in the first place, not to consider this something bad. Rather, be sure that we must undergo temptations. God wills this so that we might have opportunities to practice the different virtues and not grow careless in the spiritual life. Scripture teaches this clearly. The life of man, Job says, is a continual battle [Job 7:1], and Sirach says, my son, when you enter God's service, prepare your soul for temptation [Sir 2:1]. It was because you were acceptable to God, Saint Raphael says to Tobit, that it was necessary for you to be tried by temptation [Tob 12:13]. Saint Paul, after he was raised to the third heaven, had to suffer a thorn in the flesh so that his virtue might be further purified [2 Cor 12:1–9]. More than all this, the Holy One of all holy ones, Jesus Christ, also willed to undergo temptations [Mt 4:1–11]. Thus, we should consider temptations as favors and be filled with spiritual joy according to Saint James's teaching, when he says: my brother, consider that all joy in this life consists in bearing temptations, knowing that in temptation we exercise patience and, with patience, all virtue [Jas 1:2–3].[5]

Saint Thérèse of Lisieux

Recounted by her novice, Sister Marie of the Trinity:

On another occasion, she said to me, "Notice the method used to make copper objects shine: you coat them with mud, with things that make them dirty and dull. After this is done, they shine like gold. Well, temptations are like this mud for the soul. They only serve

[5] *If You Want Peace in This Life: The Spiritual Letters of Venerable Bruno Lanteri*, trans. Timothy Gallagher, O.M.V. (EWTN Publishing, 2025), 7.

to make it shine with the virtues opposed to those very temptations."[6]

The Lord permits, Ignatius says, a person to undergo desolation "so that he may resist the various agitations and temptations of the enemy", thereby growing in the spiritual life.

In a letter to her sister Céline:

St. Teresa says we must maintain love. *The wood* is not within our reach when we are in darkness, in aridities, but at least are we not obliged to throw little pieces of straw on it? Jesus is really powerful enough to keep the fire going by Himself. However, He is satisfied when He sees us put a little fuel on it. . . .

I want at least to tell Him frequently that I love Him; this is not difficult, and it keeps the *fire* going. *Even though* this fire of love would seem to me to have gone out, I would like to throw something on it, and Jesus could then relight it.[7]

Céline comments on this letter: "She was never discouraged. She sometimes felt weak or spiritually dry, but this made her only all the more faithful to the practice of virtue."[8]

Jean-Pierre de Caussade, S.J.

It is true that a canvas simply and blindly offered to the brush feels at each moment only the stroke of the brush. It is the same with a lump of stone. Each blow from the

[6] *"Le carnet rouge de soeur Marie de la Trinité"*, Les Archives du Carmel de Lisieux, no. 51, author's translation, https://archives.carmeldelisieux.fr/au-carmel-du-temps-de-therese/la-communaute/soeur-marie-de-la-trinite/documents-soeur-marie-de-la-trinite/le-carnet-rouge-de-soeur-marie-de-la-trinite/.

[7] *Letters of St. Thérèse of Lisieux*, trans. John Clarke, O.C.D., vol. 2, *1890–1897* (ICS Publications, 1988), 801.

[8] *St. Thérèse of Lisieux by Those Who Knew Her*, ed. and trans. Christopher Maloney, O.C.D. (Veritas Publications, 1975), 126.

hammering of the sculptor's chisel makes it feel—if it could—as if it were being destroyed. As blow after blow descends, the stone knows nothing of how the sculptor is shaping it. All it feels is a chisel chopping away at it, cutting it and mutilating it. For example, let's take a piece of stone destined to be carved into a crucifix or a statue. We might ask it: "What do you think is happening to you?" And it might answer: "Don't ask me. All I know is that I must stay immovable in the hands of the sculptor, and I must love him and endure all he inflicts on me to produce the figure he has in mind. He knows how to do it. As for me, I have no idea what he is doing, nor do I know what he will make of me. But what I do know is that his work is the best possible. It is perfect. I welcome each blow of his chisel as the best thing that could happen to me, although, if I'm to be truthful, I feel that every one of these blows is ruining me, destroying me, and disfiguring me. But I remain unconcerned. I concentrate on the present moment, think only of my duty, and suffer all that this master sculptor inflicts on me without knowing his purpose or fretting about it."

Yes, you frank and precious souls, leave to God what is his business, and carry on peacefully with your work.[9]

"Let one who is in desolation consider how the Lord has left him in trial."

Thomas à Kempis

I have never found any religious man who has not experienced at times a diminishment of grace or felt a lessening of fervor; nor any saint, no matter how high he was raised

[9] *Abandonment to Divine Providence*, trans. John Beevers (Image Books, 1975), 82.

or enlightened who was not, sooner or later, visited by temptation. No one is worthy of contemplating the high things of God who has not, for God, been tried by trials. Commonly, the trial that precedes it is a sign of the consolation to follow. Heavenly consolation is promised to those who undergo trials. To the one who overcomes, the Lord says, I will give to eat of the tree of life [Rev 2:7].[10]

Pope Francis

The history of salvation is worked out "in hope against hope" (Rom 4:18), through our weaknesses. All too often, we think that God works only through our better parts, yet most of his plans are realized in and despite our frailty. Thus Saint Paul could say: "To keep me from being too elated, a thorn was given me in the flesh, a messenger of Satan to torment me, to keep me from being too elated. Three times I appealed to the Lord about this, that it would leave me, but he said to me: 'My grace is sufficient for you, for power is made perfect in weakness'" (2 Cor 12:7–9).

Since this is part of the entire economy of salvation, we must learn to look upon our weaknesses with tender mercy.[11]

Saint Rose of Lima

Let all men know that grace comes after tribulation. Let them know that without the burden of afflictions it is

[10] *De Imitatione Christi*, bk. 2, chap. 9, author's translation.

[11] Apostolic letter *Patris Corde* (December 8, 2020), no. 2, https://www.vatican.va/content/francesco/en/apost_letters/documents/papa-francesco-lettera-ap_20201208_patris-corde.html.

impossible to reach the height of grace. Let them know that gifts of grace increase as the struggles increase....

No one would complain about his cross or about troubles that may happen to him, if he would come to know the scales on which they are weighed when they are distributed to men.[12]

Saint Teresa of Avila

On prayer:

So I return to the advice—and even if I repeat it many times this doesn't matter—that it is very important that no one be distressed or afflicted over dryness or noisy and distracting thoughts. If a person wishes to gain freedom of spirit and not be always troubled, let him begin by not being frightened by the cross, and he will see how the Lord also helps him carry it and he will gain satisfaction and profit from everything.[13]

"Because he can resist with the divine help, which always remains with him".

Whoever lives in the presence of so good a friend and excellent a leader, who went ahead of us to be the first to suffer, can endure all things. The Lord helps us, strengthens us, and never fails; He is a true friend.[14]

[12] Quoted in *The Liturgy of the Hours*, vol. 4 (Catholic Book Publishing, 1975), 1342.

[13] *The Book of Her Life*, in *The Collected Works of St. Teresa of Avila*, trans. Kieran Kavanaugh, O.C.D., and Otilio Rodriguez, O.C.D., vol. 1 (ICS Publications, 1976), 85.

[14] *Collected Works*, 1:146. These two quotations from St. Teresa of Avila are cited in Darío López Tejada, S.J., *Los ejercicios espirituales de San Ignacio de Loyola: Comentario y textos afines* (Edibesa, 1998), 865–66.

John the Serene (Bishop)

In a sermon:

We should then in the fullest sense not only with our voice but with our very soul cry out, *The Lord is my light and my salvation; whom shall I fear?* If he enlightens and saves me, whom shall I fear? Even though the dark shadows of evil suggestions crowd about, *the Lord is my light.* They can approach, but cannot prevail; they can lay siege to our heart, but cannot conquer it. Though the blindness of concupiscence assails us, again we say: *The Lord is my light.* For he is our strength; he gives himself to us and we give ourselves to him.[15]

Lorenzo Scupoli, C.R.

On the four means of acquiring confidence in God:

First. To ask it with great humility.

Second. To contemplate with an ardent faith the immense power and infinite wisdom of the Supreme Being. To him nothing is difficult; his goodness is unlimited. . . .

Third. Frequently to recall what we are assured of in the Holy Scriptures, the witnesses of truth, in a thousand different places—that no one who puts his trust in God will be defeated.

Fourth. The final means of acquiring both distrust of self and confidence in God is that before attempting to perform any good action, or to encounter some failing, we should look at our own weakness on the one hand, and on the

[15] Quoted in *The Liturgy of the Hours*, vol. 3 (Catholic Book Publishing, 1975), 130–31.

other contemplate the infinite power, wisdom, and goodness of God. Balancing what we fear from ourselves with what we hope from God, we shall courageously undergo the greatest difficulties and severest trials.[16]

Walter Hilton (Fourteenth-Century English Augustinian Writer)

On responding to temptations:

The remedies for such may be these. First: that they put all their trust in our Lord Jesus Christ, and often call to mind his Passion and the pains that he suffered for us, and that they then believe steadfastly that all sorrows and travail that they suffer in such temptations, which to unskillful men may seem a forsaking by God, are indeed no such leavings or forsakings, but trials for their good, either for the cleansing of their former sins or for the great increasing of their reward and the disposing of them for more grace, if they will but suffer awhile and stand fast, that they turn not again willingly to sin.

Another remedy is that they fear not, nor esteem these malicious stirrings for sins, nor lay to heart that despair or blasphemy, or doubtings of sacrament, or any such other, though never so ugly to hear; for the feeling of these temptations defiles the soul no more than if they heard a hound bark or felt the biting of a flea. They vex the soul indeed, but do not harm it, if so be a man despise them and set them at nought.[17]

[16] *The Spiritual Combat and a Treatise on Peace of the Soul*, trans. William Lester and Robert Mohan (Newman Press,1958), 11–13.

[17] *The Scale (or Ladder) of Perfection*, chap. 2, https://www.ccel.org/ccel/h/hilton/ladder/cache/ladder.pdf.

Saint Pierre Favre

Note here, O my soul, how our Lord drew you out of great spiritual tribulations and distress caused by the severe temptations you endured because of your defects and also because of the turmoil stirred up by the spirit of fornication and because of your negligence in bearing fruit.

Remember the very clear understanding you received about the causes of those temptations. Remember that you almost never had a grievous temptation without finding consolation not only through clear knowledge but also through a spirit contrary to the melancholy moods, the fears, the fits of discouragement, or the dejection that succeeds illusory hopes. For our Lord gave you a very clear knowledge and genuine feelings to serve you as remedies against the spirit of fornication and as means of purifying the flesh and the spirit. These he gave you as remedies and as means to resist the world and its spirits and others as a defense against evil spirits.[18]

"Because he can resist with the divine help, which always remains with him".

Saint John Vianney

During the harvest season the harvesters rise early and work hard, but they do not complain, since it is a question of making money. Temptation is the season of spiritual harvest.[19]

[18] *The Memoriale*, in *The Spiritual Writings of Pierre Favre*, trans. Edmond Murphy, S.J., and Martin Palmer, S.J. (Institute of Jesuit Sources, 1996), 82–83.

[19] *Thoughts of the Curé d'Ars*, "On Temptations", Kindle, loc. 398.

He also said, "Whoever has not experienced temptation cannot enter into the Kingdom of Heaven." He even added, "Without temptations no one can be saved."[20]

Pseudo-Macarius (Anonymous Author of Spiritual Writings in Early Christian Times)

The mind and intellect of Christians are always centered on heavenly thoughts. They gazed on heavenly things because they participate in the Holy Spirit. Because they have been born above from God and are children of God in truth and power, they have arrived, through many labors and sweat endured over a long time, at a state of equilibrium, tranquillity and peace, freed from further sifting. They no longer vacillate back and forth, tossed about by crippling and vain thoughts.[21]

Through the trial of spiritual desolation, we grow stronger.

Jules Toner, S.J.

No one can grow as a Christian without any spiritual consolation, that is true; but it is also true that without spiritual

[20] *The Sayings of the Desert Fathers*, trans. Benedicta Ward, S.L.G. (Cistercian Publications, 1984), 2.

[21] Pseudo-Macarius, *The Fifty Spiritual Homilies and the "Great Letter"*, ed. and trans. George A. Maloney, S.J. (Paulist Press, 1992), 64. "Pseudo-Macarius" is the title given to the anonymous author of spiritual works written before the mid-sixth century and, until more recent scholarship placed this in doubt, attributed to the fourth-century figure of holiness Macarius of Egypt.

desolation, we who are wounded by original sin would likely remain shallow—children, so to speak, spiritually spoiled.[22]

[22] *A Commentary on Saint Ignatius' Rules for the Discernment of Spirits: A Guide to the Principles and Practice* (Institute of Jesuit Sources, 1982), 188. For complementary quotations, see Timothy M. Gallagher, O.M.V., *The Discernment of Spirits: An Ignatian Guide for Everyday Living* (Crossroad, 2005): St. Angela of Foligno (95–96), St. Ignatius (102), St. Teresa of Avila (102).

Rule 8

Be Still

In rule 8, Ignatius continues to supply remedies for spiritual desolation. He writes:

> **Eighth Rule.** Let one who is in desolation work to be in patience, which is contrary to the vexations that come to him, and let him think that he will soon be consoled, diligently using the means against such desolation, as is said in the sixth rule.

In this rule, Ignatius offers three mutually strengthening aids for one struggling with spiritual desolation. This person is (1) to "work to be in patience", (2) to "think that he will soon be consoled", and (3) to use diligently "the means against such desolation, as is said in the sixth rule".

Work to Be in Patience

The key virtue, Ignatius says, in time of spiritual desolation is *patience*: Let the one who is in desolation "trabaje de estar en paciencia" (work to be in patience).[1] Such patience is "contrary to the vexations that come to him", which urge

[1] *San Ignacio de Loyola: Obras* (Biblioteca de Autores Cristianos, 2013), 224.

him to surrender to discouragement, to relinquish prayer, and to abandon his new spiritual steps. The word *patience*, from the Latin *patior*, means "the ability to bear, to endure, to suffer, to undergo". This is the person who *will not give up* in time of spiritual desolation, who stays the course and remains faithful, completing his daily prayer, attending the Bible study, and avoiding the temptation to flee into "low and earthly things". The verb *trabajar* (to work) indicates that this requires courage and effort. Saint Teresa of Avila famously writes, "Patience obtains all things."[2]

Know That Consolation Is Coming

Such patience is not mere effort of will. As in the preceding rule, Ignatius calls the one in spiritual desolation to *think* in a certain way—to reflect on, call to mind, ponder a specific truth that renders this patience much easier. The person in desolation is to "think that he will *soon* be consoled". *Soon.* A powerful adverb, and the truth of the person's situation.

Spiritual desolation—that is, the enemy in time of desolation—will attempt to predict the future. It insinuates that the desolation will continue tomorrow, next week, the following week, and beyond, without foreseeable end.

If we believe the enemy's lie, the desolation will be difficult to bear. If, for example, the man at 10:00 P.M. and the woman at 4:00 P.M. believe that their desolation will last at length, they are likely to surrender to it. Against this lie, Ignatius says, let them *think*, let them call to mind,

[2] Translation of "La paciencia todo lo alcanza", in "Nada te turbe", the poem known as her "Bookmark". Provincia Carmelita, October 15, 2022, https://www.carmelitas.es/rincon-carmelita/rincon-carmelita-nada-te-turbe-santa-teresa-de-jesus-15-octubre-2022.

the truth: first, that this desolation will pass; second, that consolation will return; and third, that it will return much sooner than the desolation would have them believe. Thinking of this truth, they will more easily remain patient and steadfast in the time of desolation.

Those who practice rule 8 experience its encouragement, and in full measure if they also adhere to its third part.

Be Diligent

Thoughts are vitally important in resisting spiritual desolation, but their impact is greater when joined to action. As in rule 6, Ignatius again calls those in desolation to apply with *diligence*—with energy, with hope, with confidence—the four means proposed there: (1) prayer of petition, (2) meditation on truths that sustain, (3) attentive examination of the experience, and (4) suitable gestures of penitential courage.

The effort to remain patient in desolation, the thought that consolation will return soon, and the practice of the four means just named supply, in combination, a formidable weapon against desolation.

This, Too, Shall Pass

Do you know those mornings when you rise and everything seems gray, when the whole day ahead seems bathed in gloom? They are rule-8 mornings! When I feel this upon rising, I remember rule 8: that desolation's claim over the day is a lie, that consolation will return soon. And every time, I find that rule 8 is true. Often, just remembering rule 8 banishes the desolation.

Ignatius reminds us that we will "soon be consoled". After a surgery, the doctor told me that I would feel some pain for two or three days but that it would then pass. It was painful for those first days, but knowing that it would pass soon made it much easier to bear. The false claim of spiritual desolation over the future is that the desolation will just go on and on. Ignatius wants to unmask this claim in rule 8: We will "soon be consoled". He is right. The desolation, never lasts as long as the enemy would have us believe, especially when we employ the means to reject it.

Underlying rule 8 is Ignatius' understanding that the spiritual life consists of alternations of spiritual consolation (which pass, but leave their blessing) and spiritual desolation (which we are called to resist, and which also pass). I love sharing this truth. People say, in varying ways, "I'm normal. I'm not the only one. This is universal spiritual experience, and I can understand it and respond to it, accepting the first and rejecting the second." Yes, every one of us experiences times of spiritual consolation and spiritual desolation. We are all brothers and sisters in this, and we are all called to the liberation of the discerning life.

In recent years, I have come to appreciate much more deeply the importance and helpfulness of rules 7 and 8. Consider in time of spiritual desolation that you *can* resist (rule 7), and, in time of desolation, remember that it will pass *much sooner* than it would have you believe (rule 8).

Witnesses to Rule 8

Saint Thomas Aquinas

On patience as a virtue:

The moral virtues are directed to the good, inasmuch as they safeguard the good of reason against the impulse of the passions. Now among the passions sorrow is strong to hinder the good of reason, according to 2 Corinthians 7:10, "The sorrow of the world produces death," and Sirach 30:25, "Sadness has killed many, and there is no profit in it." Hence the necessity for a virtue to safeguard the good of reason against sorrow, lest reason give way to sorrow: and this patience does. Wherefore Augustine says (*De Patientia* ii): "A man's patience it is whereby he bears evil with an equal mind", that is, without being disturbed by sorrow, "lest he abandon with an unequal mind the goods whereby he may advance to better things".[3]

Such patience, which assists us to overcome the sorrow of spiritual desolation, is the key virtue in time of desolation.

Saint Peter Damian

The Scriptures reassure us: let your understanding strengthen your patience. In serenity look forward to the joy that follows sadness.[4]

"Let one who is in desolation work to be in patience, . . . and let him think that he will soon be consoled."

Saint Cyprian

Patience is a precept for salvation given us by our Lord, our teacher: *Whoever endures to the end will be saved.* And again: *If you persevere in my word, you will truly be my disciples; you will know the truth, and the truth will set you free.*

[3] *Summa Theologica*, trans. Fathers of the English Dominican Province, vol. 3 (Christian Classics, 1981), II-II, q. 136, a.1, co., p. 1744. I have lightly adapted the biblical quotations in keeping with contemporary usage.

[4] Quoted in *The Liturgy of the Hours*, vol. 2 (Catholic Book Publishing, 1975), 1683.

Dear brethren, we must endure and persevere if we are to attain the truth and freedom we have been allowed to hope for; faith and hope are the very meaning of our being Christians, but if faith and hope are to bear their fruit, patience is necessary.[5]

Saint Francis of Assisi

1. *Blessed are the peacemakers for they shall be called the children of God* (Mt 5:9). The servant of God cannot know how much patience and humility he has within himself as long as everything goes well with him. 2. But when the time comes in which those who should do him justice do quite the opposite to him, he has only as much patience and humility as he has on that occasion and no more.[6]

Venerable Bruno Lanteri

Begin your meditation with desire and love. Never omit it, nor shorten it, because of tedium or distractions. An ounce of prayer made with patience is worth more than one hundred pounds of prayer when you feel fervent, because of the heroic acts you practice in the first and the danger of vanity in the second. This is a maxim of St. Francis de Sales.[7]

[5] "On the Value of Patience", quoted in *The Liturgy of the Hours*, vol. 1 (Catholic Book Publishing, 1975), 192.

[6] "The Admonitions", in *Francis and Clare: The Complete Works*, trans. Regis J. Armstrong, O.F.M. Cap., and Ignatius C. Brady, O.F.M. (Paulist Press, 1982), 32.

[7] *Pio Bruno Lanteri: Scritti e documenti d'archivio*, vol. 1 (Edizioni Lanteri, 2002), 747, author's translation.

Pope Francis

Do not fear desolation; face it with perseverance, do not evade it. And in desolation, try to find the heart of Christ, to find the Lord. And the answer will come, always.[8]

Saint Augustine

You have entered upon a time of trial but you will come to no harm—God's help will bring you through it safely. You are like a piece of pottery, shaped by instruction, fired by tribulation. When you are put into the oven, therefore, keep your thoughts on the time when you will be taken out again; for God is faithful, and he will guard both your going in and your coming out.[9]

Compare "Keep your thoughts on the time when you will be taken out again" to Ignatius' "Let him think that he will soon be consoled."

George Herbert

> Yet take Thy way, for sure Thy way is best:
> Stretch or contract me, Thy poor debtor:
> This is but tuning of my breast,
> To make the music better.[10]

[8] General Audience, Catechesis on Discernment 8 (November 16, 2022), https://www.vatican.va/content/francesco/en/audiences/2022/documents/20221116-udienza-generale.html.

[9] Sermon, quoted in *The Liturgy of the Hours*, vol. 4 (Catholic Book Publishing, 1975), 609.

[10] "The Temper (1)", Poetry Foundation, https://www.poetryfoundation.org/poems/44374/the-temper-i.

Stretch (spiritual consolation) or contract (spiritual desolation) me: This is but God's spiritual tuning "to make the music better", to give me growth in my spiritual life.

Julian of Norwich

During our lifetime here we have in us a marvellous mixture of both well-being and woe. We have in us our risen Lord Jesus Christ, and we have in us the wretchedness and the harm of Adam's falling. Dying, we are constantly protected by Christ, and by the touching of his grace we are raised to true trust in salvation. And we are so afflicted in our feelings by Adam's falling in various ways, by sin and by different pains, and in this we are made dark and so blind that we can scarcely accept any comfort. But in our intention we wait for God, and trust faithfully to have mercy and grace; and this is his own working in us, and in his goodness he opens the eye of our understanding, by which we have sight, sometimes more and sometimes less, according to the ability God gives us to receive. And now we are raised to the one, and now we are permitted to fall to the other. And so that mixture is so marvellous in us that we scarcely know, about ourselves or about our fellow Christians, what condition we are in, these conflicting feelings are so extraordinary, except for each holy act of assent to God which we make when we feel him, truly willing with all our heart to be with him, and with all our soul and with all our might. And then we hate and despise our evil inclinations, and everything which could be an occasion of spiritual and bodily sin. And even so, when this sweetness is hidden, we fall again into blindness, and so in various ways into woe and tribulation. But then this is our comfort, that we know in our faith that by the power of Christ who is our protector we never assent to that, but we complain about it, and endure in pain and in woe, praying until the time that he shows himself again to us. And so we remain in this mixture all the days of our life; but he wants us to trust that he is constantly with us.[11]

Yes, we do remain in this mixture all the days of our life, and this is how we progress: accepting in time of spiritual consolation and rejecting in time of spiritual desolation.

Thomas à Kempis

When consolation is withdrawn, do not quickly despair, but with humility and patience, await the heavenly visitation, because God has power to give you again greater grace and consolation. These alternations are not strange or foreign to those who are experienced in the ways of God, who often employed such variations in his workings with the great saints and ancient prophets. Thus a certain man said, in a time of such grace, I said in my abundance that I shall never be moved [Ps 30:7]. When, however, the grace that he experienced was removed, he added, You turned your face from me, and I was troubled [Ps 30:8]. But he never despaired in these fluctuations, but all the more begged of God and said, To you, Lord, I will cry, and to my God will I make my petition [Ps 30:9]. Then he shared the fruit of his prayer and witnessed to God's answer, saying, The Lord heard me and had mercy on me. The Lord has made himself my helper [Ps 30:11]. How did the Lord answer him? You have changed, he

[11] *Julian of Norwich: Showings*, trans. Edmund Colledge, O.S.A., and James Walsh, S.J. (Paulist Press, 1978), 279–80. Ignatius also speaks of a "tranquil time" when we are neither in spiritual consolation nor in spiritual desolation. See the chapter on rule 5 in this book.

says, my sorrow into joy, and you surrounded me with joy [Ps 30:12].[12]

"These alternations are not strange or foreign to those who are experienced in the ways of God." No, they are not. And Saint Ignatius traces for us the sure path through these alternations.

[12] *De Imitatione Christi*, bk. 2, chap. 9, author's translation. The biblical citations follow the translation of the Latin Vulgate. See also the Douay-Rheims Bible. For complementary quotations, see Timothy M. Gallagher, O.M.V., *The Discernment of Spirits: An Ignatian Guide for Everyday Living* (Crossroad, 2005): Servant of God Elisabeth Leseur (104–5), Julian of Norwich (110–11); Timothy M. Gallagher, O.M.V., *Setting Captives Free: Personal Reflections on Ignatian Discernment of Spirits* (Crossroad, 2018): Caryll Houselander (154), Joannes Tauler (154).

Rule 9

Remember What Causes Desolation

In rule 9, Ignatius addresses a key question: Why does a God who loves us, and whom we seek, to love in return, permit us to undergo spiritual desolation that he could spare us? This question is not abstract. Who among us has not raised it when in darkness and, at times, with urgency and from deep pain? Ignatius raises and answers this question for practical reasons: If we understand why God permits the present desolation and the fruit he desires to give if we resist it, we will be greatly strengthened in our resistance.

He writes:

> **Ninth Rule.** There are three principal causes for which we find ourselves desolate. The first is because we are tepid, slothful, or negligent in our spiritual exercises, and so through our faults spiritual consolation withdraws from us. The second, to try us and see how much we are and how much we extend ourselves in his service and praise without so much payment of consolations and increased graces. The third, to give us true recognition and understanding so that we may interiorly feel that it is not ours to attain or maintain increased devotion, intense love, tears, or any other spiritual consolation, but that all is the gift and grace of God our Lord, and so that we may not build a nest in something belonging to another, raising our mind

in some pride or vainglory, attributing to ourselves the devotion or the other parts of the spiritual consolation.

"There are *three principal causes* for which we find ourselves desolate." In this context, *cause* signifies God's reason in permitting this spiritual desolation: the fruit, the growth, he desires to give if we resist and reject the desolation. Should the man at 10:00 P.M. and the woman at 4:00 P.M. not resist the desolation, it will bring no fruit but work the harm for which the enemy hopes. If, however, they resist and reject it, then blessed fruits enter their spiritual lives, fruits that would not be gained otherwise. Ignatius describes three such fruits.

Our Faults and Conversion

When, Ignatius says, "we are tepid, slothful, or negligent in our spiritual exercises"—that is, in one or another aspect of our spiritual lives—God may permit spiritual desolation as a wake-up call to eliminate that regression. The man prays for twenty minutes every morning and loves the closeness with the Lord this brings. The woman goes to daily Mass and knows how this blesses her day. Recently, the man has omitted this prayer and the woman her daily Mass. God may allow spiritual desolation, Ignatius affirms, to alert them to the slippage and to nudge them to renew these beneficial practices. This is a God, Ignatius writes, "who loves me more than I love myself"[1] and who will permit spiritual desolation to help us overcome negligence

[1] "Spiritual Diary", April 2, 1544, quoted in Simon Decloux, S.J., *Commentaries on the Letters and Spiritual Diary of St. Ignatius Loyola* (Centrum Ignatianum Spiritualitatis, 1983), 173.

so that these areas of our spiritual lives will be directed toward him, as we ourselves desire.

A Trial and Growth

Ignatius, however, does not equate every experience of spiritual desolation with faults on our part. The second and third reasons God may allow spiritual desolation have nothing to do with such faults but rather with the further growth that normally is given only through the trial of desolation.

He continues, "The second [is] to *try us* and *see* how much we are and how much we extend ourselves in his service and praise without so much payment of consolations and increased graces." As in rule 7, Ignatius refers to spiritual desolation as a *trial*. From this trial, something is *seen*—something is learned. If we resist the desolation, this trial will bring spiritual growth, progress, and increased wisdom.

The man and the woman undergo some days of spiritual desolation. They are discerning, and they identify the desolation for the tactic of the enemy that it is. They refuse to change their proposals (rule 5); they turn to prayer, meditation, examination, and suitable penance (rule 6); they reflect that they can overcome this desolation with God's sufficient grace (rule 7); and they remember that consolation will return sooner than the desolation would have them believe (rule 8). Both emerge from the desolation not only unharmed but also stronger to resist such desolation in the future, more confident in God's accompanying love and grace. We have quoted the author who affirms that without desolation, we would remain spiritual children.[2] God, "who loves us more than we love ourselves", loves us too much to allow this.

The Grace of Consolation and Humility

In time of spiritual consolation, we may tend to ascribe the consolation more to our own efforts than to God's grace. For Ignatius, the rich biblical space of humility (Mt 5:3; 11:29; Lk 1:48) opens us to all growth in the spiritual life.[3] Its contrary, with its accompanying self-dependence and overconfidence, closes that door. Thus, Ignatius says, God may allow spiritual desolation to help root us in humility. The time of spiritual desolation, when we experience its burden and struggle to resist it, teaches us "in the flesh" that all spiritual consolation is the gift of God's grace.

Ignatius writes:

> The third [is] to give us true recognition and understanding so that we may interiorly feel that it is not ours to attain or maintain increased devotion, intense love, tears, or any other spiritual consolation, but that all is the gift and grace of God our Lord, and so that we may not build a nest in something belonging to another, raising our mind in some pride or vainglory, attributing to ourselves the devotion or the other parts of the spiritual consolation.

Why, then, does a God who loves us permit us to undergo spiritual desolation that he could spare us? Ignatius answers: because of a love that brings us healing from

[2] Jules Toner, S.J., *A Commentary on Saint Ignatius' Rules for the Discernment of Spirits: A Guide to the Principles and Practice* (Institute of Jesuit Sources, 1982), 188.

[3] *SpirEx* 146.

regression (first reason), gives us growth toward spiritual maturity (second reason), and helps us avoid the pitfall of self-dependence apart from his grace (third reason). Said more simply, God uses the enemy's tactic of spiritual desolation against the enemy who brings it.

Witnesses to Rule 9

Jules Toner, S.J.

If God withdraws consolation that he could continue to give and allows desolation that he could prevent, it can only be because at certain times in our lives he sees desolation serving his loving aims for our good better than consolation would.[4]

Saint Jerome Emiliani

On why God allows us to struggle, in a letter dated June 21, 1535:

God alone knows the reason for all this, yet we can recognize three causes; in the first place, our blessed Lord is telling you that he desires to include you among his beloved sons, provided that you remain steadfast in his ways, for this is the way he treats his friends and makes them holy.

The second reason is that he is asking you to grow continually in your confidence in him alone....

Now there is a third reason. God wishes to test you like gold in the furnace. The dross is consumed by the fire, but

[4] Toner, *Commentary*, 185.

the pure gold remains and its value increases. It is in this manner that God acts with his good servant, who puts his hope in him and remains unshaken in times of distress. God raises him up and, in return for the things he has left out of love for God, he repays him a hundredfold in this life and eternal life hereafter.[5]

Saint Pierre Favre

From his journal:

In his justice and mercy, therefore, God sends you such trials for a time or permits them because you were so indifferent to his good gifts; then, to prevent your becoming lukewarm and apathetic, he leaves you with stings and goads to drive you ceaselessly forward until at last you find rest in God our Lord. . . .

Do not be content, therefore, that you do not descend, that you neither decrease nor go back; but "dispose your heart to ascend" [Ps 84:6], to increase and to make interior progress not through fear of descending or going back or falling but through love of holiness.[6]

Saint Thomas Aquinas

Commenting on the verses "I am the true vine, and my Father is the vinedresser. Every branch of mine that bears

[5] Quoted in *The Liturgy of the Hours*, vol. 2 (Catholic Book Publishing, 1976), 1370–71.

[6] *The Memoriale*, in *The Spiritual Writings of Pierre Favre*, trans. Edmond Murphy, S.J., and Martin Palmer, S.J. (Institute of Jesuit Sources, 1996), 99.

no fruit, he takes away, and every branch that does bear fruit he prunes, that it may bear more fruit" (Jn 15:1–2):

His interest in the good branches is to help them so they can bear more fruit. So he says, *and every branch that does bear fruit he prunes, that it may bear more fruit.* Considering the literal sense, we see that a natural vine with branches that has many shoots bears less fruit, because the sap is spread out through all the shoots. Thus the vinedresser prunes away the extra shoots so that the vine can bear more fruit. It is the same with us. For if we are well-disposed and united to God, yet scatter our love over many things, our virtue becomes weak and we become less able to do good. This is why God, in order that we may bear fruit, will frequently remove such obstacles and prune us by sending troubles and temptations, which make us stronger. Accordingly, he says, he *prunes*, even though one may be clean, for in this life no one is so clean that he does not need to be cleansed more and more.... And he does this *so that it may bear more fruit*, that is, grow in virtue.[7]

Saint Alphonsus Liguori

"God is faithful," says the apostle Paul, "and he will not let you be tested beyond your strength, but with the testing he will also provide the way out so that you may be able to endure it" (1 Cor 10:13). Thus a person who resists temptation not only loses nothing by it, but profits greatly

[7] *Commentary on the Gospel of John, Chapter 15*, https://isidore.co/aquinas/english/John15.htm. Reginald Garrigou-Lagrange cites this text in *The Three Ages of the Interior Life: Prelude of Eternal Life*, trans. M. Timothea Doyle, vol. 1 (Catholic Way, 2014), 187–88, italics in original.

("with the temptations he will also provide the way of escape"). That is why God often allows the souls dearest to him to be the most tried by temptations, that they may acquire more merit on this earth and more glory in heaven. Stagnant water soon goes bad; and souls that stand idle, without any temptations and combats, are in danger of perishing from vain complacency about their own merit; perhaps they think they have already reached perfection, and so have little fear, seldom commend themselves to God, and make little effort to secure their salvation. But when they are shaken by temptations and see themselves in danger of plunging into sin, then they have recourse to God and to the divine Mother; they renew their resolution to die rather than to sin; they humble themselves and abandon themselves to the embrace of God's mercy. In this way as experience shows, the soul grows stronger and comes closer to God.[8]

Saint John Henry Newman

Speaking of King David's fidelity followed by lapses:

And if these things be so in the case of the favoured saints of God, what (may we suppose) is our own real spiritual state in His sight? It is a serious thought. The warning to be deduced from it is this:—Never to think we have a due knowledge of ourselves till we have been exposed to various kinds of temptations, and tried on every side. Integrity on one side of our character is no voucher for integrity on another. We cannot tell how we should act

[8] *The Practice of the Love of Jesus Christ* (Liguori Publications, 1999), 188.

if brought under temptations different from those which we have hitherto experienced. This thought should keep us humble.[9]

Saint Philip Neri

The fervor of spirituality is usually very great in the beginning, but afterward, the Lord *fingit se longius ire* [Lk 24:28], makes as though he would go farther: in such a case we must stand firm and not be disturbed, because God is then withdrawing his most holy hand of sweetnesses, to see if we are strong; and then, if we resist and overcome those tribulations and temptations, the sweetnesses and heavenly consolations return.[10]

Compare Ignatius' "The second [is] to try us and see how much we are and how much we extend ourselves in his service and praise without so much payment of consolations and increased graces."

Saint Charles of Sezze

On this sea of disturbances I was like a ship without rigging, without oars and sails, battered by the storm, guided only by the providence and counsel of God. When he wants us to accomplish great and important things, it is not his way to allow everything to go along very gently and smoothly; rather to ensure that we embrace these tasks with great determination, he permits difficulties to

[9] "Sermon 4: Secret Faults", in *Parochial and Plain Sermons*, vol. 1, https://www.newmanreader.org/works/parochial/volume1/sermon4.html.

[10] *The Maxims and Sayings of St. Philip Neri*, trans. F. W. Faber (St. Athanasius Press, 2009), September 3, Kindle, loc. 261–65.

arise so that what we do will be well grounded on the rock of virtue.[11]

Venerable Bruno Lanteri

Forgive me if I have not replied to your letter earlier, but this was not possible for me. I carried out your commission, and you have no reason to be troubled. You would like to live already in heaven, where there are no longer ups and downs, but you need patience, since you are still here below, and you need to bear with patience the trials necessary to go to heaven.[12]

Servant of God Elisabeth Leseur

My Savior, I am all alone spiritually, as you know. You know, too, how I suffer from the hostility or indifference of certain persons. I think that is why you have done so much for me and given me so much in your goodness. And now with your gentle gaze you are dispersing the clouds that in these last months have so often overshadowed me. You are kindling my heart again after leaving it in painful dryness; you are chasing away the darkness and the confusion. Thank you, my beloved Savior, my God! I know that sorrow will return, for effort and struggle are your will for us. Your love has conquered, and I know that you will not abandon me and that deep peace will remain with me. To love during

[11] *St. Charles of Sezze: Autobiography*, ed. and trans. Leonard Perotti, O.F.M. (Burns & Oates, 1963), 28.

[12] *Carteggio del Venerabile Padre Pio Bruno Lanteri (1759–1830)*, ed. Paolo Calliari, O.M.V., vol. 3 (Editrice Lanteriana, 1976), 164–65, author's translation.

the storm is very consoling, and my love grows stronger after each sorrow, each setback. Complete abandonment to you, offering my heart and my life in your service.[13]

Saint Catherine of Siena

In times of struggle we come to know ourselves and our weakness better. And we come to know God's goodness within us better when we see that God has graciously preserved our good and holy will—and it is the will alone that sins or merits. So you see how in times of intense struggle we become more perfect and prove ourselves in virtue.[14]

The second reason: a trial from which blessed learning arises.

Only when discernment is rooted in humility is it virtuous, producing life-giving fruit and willingly yielding what is due to everyone....

Without this humility, as I have said, the soul would be without discernment. For lack of discernment is set in pride, just as discernment is set in humility....

If you have this virtue [discernment], then whatever your state in life may be ... all that you do for your neighbors will be done with discernment and loving charity. For discernment and charity are engrafted together and planted in the soil of that true humility that is born of self-knowledge.[15]

[13] *Elisabeth Leseur: Selected Writings*, trans. Janet Ruffing, R.S.M. (Paulist Press, 2005), 119–20.

[14] *The Letters of Catherine of Siena*, trans. Suzanne Noffke, O.P., vol. 2 (Arizona Center for Medieval and Renaissance Studies, 2001), 648.

[15] *Catherine of Siena: The Dialogue*, trans. Suzanne Noffke, O.P. (Paulist Press, 1980), 40–41.

Yes, only when discernment is wedded to humility is it true discernment. This has become increasingly apparent to me over the years. Such is, Ignatius says, the third reason God may permit spiritual desolation: to help us live with a humility "that leads to all the other virtues".[16]

Servant of God Walter Ciszek

"My yoke is sweet and my burden light" [Mt 11:28], said Christ.... Can there be anything more consoling than to look at a burden, or a humiliation, not just as it is in itself but as the will of God entrusted to you at that moment? Viewed in that way, no matter how heavy or trying the burden or the difficulty, I am able to carry it in a spirit that indeed can make it light, for the realization that it comes from God and is his will for me carries with it a feeling of enthusiasm, of accomplishment, of importance, that brings joy and consolation to the heart.[17]

Thomas à Kempis

If, while praying and meditating on God's good gifts, you find yourself spiritually sad, cold, and dry, do not yield to despondency, nor should you cease calling humbly on Jesus. Rather, in your poverty of spirit, offer praise and thanks to God; and in your search for consolation, readily recite this verse: "The poor and those in need will praise Your name, O Lord" [Ps 74:21].

[16] *SpirEx* 146.

[17] *He Leadeth Me* (Image Books, 1973), chap. 18, Kindle, loc. 2591.

Many a saint and many a devout individual have, at various times, experienced spiritual aridity, and over a long period of time have felt themselves abandoned by God. This was so that, by their feeling of sadness and utter need, they might learn patience and compassion for others and not to rely overmuch on themselves in periods of fervor and consolation. Together with the prophet, recite this verse from the Psalms: "A beggar am I and poor, yet the Lord cares for me" [Ps 40:17]. My trust is in the Lord, for He is my strength and salvation.[18]

A trial, so that "they might learn".

It is good for me, Lord, that you humbled me, that I might learn your just ways [Ps 119:71] and cast from myself all pride of heart and presumption.[19]

God permits spiritual desolation at times "so that we may not build a nest in something belonging to another [i.e., to God], raising our mind in some pride or vainglory, attributing to ourselves the devotion or the other parts of the spiritual consolation".

Saint Anthony of the Desert

Abba Anthony said, "I saw all the snares that the enemy spreads out over the world, and I said groaning, 'What can get through from such snares?' Then I heard a voice saying to me, 'Humility.' "[20]

[18] *Bountiful Goodness: "A Little Garden of Roses" and "The Valley of Lilies"*, trans. Joseph N. Tylenda, S.J. (Ignatius Press, 2013), 92–93.

[19] *De Imitatione Christi*, bk. 3, chap. 50, author's translation.

[20] *The Sayings of the Desert Fathers: The Alphabetical Collection*, trans. Benedicta Ward, S.L.G. (Cistercian Publications, 1975), 2.

Pope Francis

Even the spiritual state we call *desolation*, when everything is dark and sad in the heart, this state of *desolation* can be an opportunity for growth. Indeed, if there is not a little dissatisfaction, a little healthy sadness, a healthy capacity to dwell in solitude and to be with ourselves without fleeing, we run the risk of always remaining on the surface of things and never making contact with the core of our existence. Desolation causes an "unrest in the soul": when one is sad it is as if the soul were shaken. It keeps us alert, it fosters vigilance and humility, and protects us from the winds of fancy. These are indispensable conditions for progress in life, and hence, also in spiritual life. . . .

Desolation is also an invitation to *gratuitousness*, to not acting always and solely with a view to emotional gratification. Being desolate offers us the possibility of growth, of initiating a more mature, more beautiful relationship with the Lord and with our loved ones.[21]

God permits spiritual desolation, Ignatius says, as a trial from which learning, growth, and progress come.

Léon Bloy

Man has recesses in his heart that were not there until pain came along to create them.[22]

[21] General Audience, Catechesis on Discernment 8 (November 16, 2022), https://www.vatican.va/content/francesco/en/audiences/2022/documents/20221116-udienza-generale.html.

[22] Quoted in José Ignacio Tellechea Idígoras, *Ignatius of Loyola: The Pilgrim Saint*, trans. Cornelius Buckley, S.J. (Loyola University Press, 1994), 125.

Joseph Tissot, M.S.F.S.

We should combat Satan with his own weapons, turn his artifices back on him, and transform into a medicine the very wounds he inflicts upon us.[23]

This is the heart of rule 9: God using the enemy's artifices (spiritual desolation) against him, transforming them into opportunities for growth and blessing.

Joseph

In Egypt, to his brothers (Gen 50:20):

You meant evil against me; but God meant it for good.[24]

The enemy intends spiritual desolation for harm; God permits it for good.

[23] *How to Profit from Your Faults: Based on the Writings of St. Francis de Sales* (Scepter, 2004), 48.

[24] For complementary quotations, see Timothy M. Gallagher, O.M.V., *The Discernment of Spirits: An Ignatian Guide for Everyday Living* (Crossroad, 2005): St. Ignatius (117–18), St. Francis of Assisi (121–22); Timothy M. Gallagher, O.M.V., *Setting Captives Free: Personal Reflections on Ignatian Discernment of Spirits* (Crossroad, 2018): St. Ignatius (171), St. Pierre Favre (172–73).

Rule 10

Use Consolation to Prepare

After five rules for the person in spiritual desolation, Ignatius turns to the person in spiritual consolation. His purpose, however, remains the same: to assist us in the struggle against desolation. In the preceding five rules, Ignatius provided tools for this struggle in time of desolation. Now he counsels us to live times of consolation, before desolation begins, in a way that will allow us to gain strength for that future struggle. Because we are prepared in advance, spiritual desolation will be much easier to resist when it returns. Ignatius' text reads:

> **Tenth Rule.** Let one who is in consolation think how he will conduct himself in the desolation that will come after, taking new strength for that time.

The primary call in time of spiritual consolation is, obviously, to receive (in the original, *recibir*) this gift, allowing God to love and strengthen us through it. Nothing, not even Ignatius' rule 10 (in time of consolation, prepare for future desolation), must ever weigh upon our freedom to accept the present consolation with a receptive and grateful heart.

A long tradition supports this claim. Saint Elizabeth Seton describes a beautiful experience of spiritual consolation:

"Then I laid still to enjoy the heavenly peace that came over my soul, and I am sure, in the two hours so enjoyed, grew ten years in the spiritual life."[1] Saint Bonaventure says of Saint Francis of Assisi, "Francis would never let any call of the Spirit go unanswered; when he experienced it, he would make the most of it and enjoy the consolation afforded him in this way for as long as God permitted it. If he was on a journey, and felt the near approach of God's Spirit, he would stop and let his companions go on, while he drank in the joy of this new inspiration; he refused to offer God's grace an ineffectual welcome."[2] Such quotations may be readily multiplied. When the man at 10:00 P.M. and the woman at 4:00 P.M. experience spiritual consolation, their primary call, like that of Elizabeth and Francis, is simply to "drink in" the gift, allowing God to love and encourage them.[3]

In the next days, however, with their hearts still warmed by the consolation, they may look ahead to the eventual return of spiritual desolation and prepare. In this way, an additional good of great value is added to the primary good of spiritual consolation.

"Let the one who is in consolation think how he will conduct himself in the desolation that will come after,

[1] Quoted in Joseph Dirvin, C.M., *Mrs. Seton: Foundress of the American Sisters of Charity* (Farrar, Strauss & Giroux, 1975), 25.

[2] St. Bonaventure, *Major Life of St. Francis*, in *St. Francis of Assisi: Writings and Early Biographies; English Omnibus of the Sources for the Life of St. Francis*, ed. Marion A. Habig (Franciscan Herald Press, 1973), 706.

[3] On St. John of the Cross and spiritual consolation: "St. John of the Cross is not speaking to all Christians indiscriminately when he counsels the rejection of sensible consolation. He is only concerned with those who are beginning to enjoy the mystic state, and he simply asks them to give it the preference when it encounters any obstacle in devotions of the sensible order and the pleasure felt in them. When no such conflict occurs, we must resort to all the means that can lead us towards God." Augustin Poulain, S.J., *The Graces of Interior Prayer* (Routledge & Kegan Paul, 1950), 405–6.

taking new strength for that time." Rule 10 contains two related calls: (1) to *think* in a certain way in a determined setting (spiritual consolation), and (2) to *take new strength* for future spiritual desolation.

Thinking in Consolation

The man experiences several days of spiritual consolation and the woman likewise. They feel God's closeness and love, prayer is alive, the sacraments draw them, the Bible speaks to their hearts, they have energy for new steps in the spiritual life, and they seek growth in their vocations. During these days of consolation, Ignatius says, let them *think*, reflect on, consider how they "will conduct" themselves, how they will respond, and what spiritual steps they will take "in the desolation that will come after".

When spiritual desolation finds us unprepared, when we have not thought in consolation about how we will conduct ourselves when it returns, we are more likely to succumb to it. Resistance is always possible—God's grace is always sufficient (rule 7)—but the struggle will be harder. When we *have* thought in consolation about future desolation and have prepared, resistance will be correspondingly easier.

Joseph, in the seven years of plenty, stores up extra grain that he does not need but that will be vital for survival in the seven years of famine that follow (Gen 41). The dynamic of rule 10 is the same.

Such thinking ahead may be done while walking, exercising, taking a long drive, sitting in church, praying the examen, journaling, or having a conversation with a spiritual guide, confessor, spouse, or spiritual friend. The blessing this will bring is evident.

This thinking is directed toward "taking new strength" to resist when desolation returns. Some suggestions follow.[4]

Pray for Strength in Future Desolation

In rule 6, Ignatius encourages such prayer in time of desolation. We need not wait, however, for desolation to pray in this manner. In days of spiritual consolation, we can ask for this strength when we face future desolation. Such prayer will be easier because of the consolation that accompanies it.

Meditate on Truths That Will Sustain You

In the same rule 6, Ignatius counseled this, too, for one in desolation. Again, we need not wait for desolation to meditate in this way. In the peace of spiritual consolation, we may reflect on, ponder, and meditate on truths of faith, scriptural verses, memories of God's fidelity in past desolation, and the like. If we do, we will find these more readily at our spiritual fingertips when we need them in desolation.

Practice Ongoing Spiritual Awareness

Again, in rule 6, Ignatius calls us to "much examination". Such examination will be easier if, in time of spiritual consolation, we practice this examination regularly. In days of

[4] See Timothy M. Gallagher, O.M.V., *The Discernment of Spirits: An Ignatian Guide for Everyday Living* (Crossroad, 2005), 133–36, where some of these suggestions are also discussed.

peaceful consolation, pray the examen prayer.[5] If journaling assists your examen, consider this as well. Choose one or more persons with whom you can speak about spiritual experience. We will return to this when we explore rule 13.

Practice a Suitable Penance

Ignatius also recommends suitable penance in time of spiritual desolation. This, too, will be easier if we do it in time of spiritual consolation. If, for example, our tendency in time of desolation is to turn to food, the smartphone or tablet, computer games, or other diversions, then in days of consolation we can practice limiting our use of them. The consolation we are experiencing will make this easier to accomplish; it will be healthy in itself, and it will prepare us to employ suitable penance in time of desolation.

Consider the Value of Desolation for Growth

On a day of spiritual consolation, we may reflect on rules 7 (God permits the trial of desolation so that we may resist and grow in the ability to resist) and 9 (three fruits that God wishes to give in permitting desolation). Such consideration will render the struggle against desolation less difficult when it recurs.

Reflect on Past Personal Growth Through Desolation

In any of the settings mentioned, in prayer, reflection, or with another person, consideration of past experiences

[5] See note 4 in the chapter on rule 6.

of desolation and how God gave growth through them renders it easier to trust that future desolation, too, will lie within God's providence and that he will offer further growth through it.

Resolve to Make No Changes in Desolation

When in spiritual consolation, recall times when you made changes to your spiritual proposals in a state of desolation. See clearly that these changes were not good. Let these memories instill in you a determination to avoid such changes during future desolation. Through this practice, the earlier changes are, in a sense, redeemed and now help you to avoid similar changes in the future.

Review the Rules

One exposure to these rules is not enough. Reading this book is not enough. Choose a way of reviewing the rules, of keeping them fresh in your awareness so they are close at hand when you need them. Create a summary of them and place it where you will see it often. Memorize a shortened form of the rules. Read about them periodically. Listen to podcasts about the rules.[6] Talk about them with others. Create digital ways of refreshing the rules. I beg of you: Take ten minutes today, or if not today, soon, to choose your way of reviewing the rules. A day will come when you will remember those ten minutes with gratitude.

[6] See Timothy Gallagher, O.M.V., "Spiritual Formation", "Fr. Timothy Gallagher: Ignatian Spirituality and More", and "Discernment of Spirits" on the Discerning Hearts app. Also available on YouTube.

Plan for Specific Situations of Desolation

If you know that a certain situation renders you vulnerable to spiritual desolation, all the more if this situation repeats, prepare ahead for it. What is that situation? When does it arise? In time of spiritual consolation, think of how you will respond when it returns. Prepare helpful ways of resisting when it does.

Find Your Sources of Strength

One winter's evening, walking back to my community's house, my heart was heavy with the burdens I was facing. As I walked, I said to the Lord, "Why is this happening? I'm just trying to do the best I can." Then this thought came: "I have been here before. This is not the first time I have felt this way, and you, Lord, have always seen me safely through these times." As I thought of this, it was easier to believe that the Lord would see me through this trial as well. My heart gently lifted. These words, "I have been here before", give me strength in desolation, all the more when I reflect on them in consolation.

What are your sources of strength? In rule 10, Ignatius invites you to see them clearly and to have them ready when spiritual desolation returns.

Witnesses to Rule 10

Walter Hilton (Fourteenth-Century English Augustinian Writer)

We are always to desire spiritual feelings of the kind I now speak of, if they come in the manner I have said before.

These are the slaying of all worldly love, the opening of the spiritual eye, purity of spirit, peace in conscience, and all the others already told. We should desire always to feel the lively inspiration of grace caused by the spiritual presence of Jesus in our soul, if we could, and to have him always with reverence in our sight; and always to feel the sweetness of his love by a wonderful homeliness of his presence. This should be our life and our feeling in grace, according to the measure of his gift in whom all grace exists; to some people more and to some less, for his presence is felt in various ways as he vouchsafes, and in this we should live and work, doing what it concerns us to do; for without this we should not know how to live. For just as the soul is the life of the body, so Jesus is the life of the soul by his gracious presence; and nevertheless this kind of feeling, however great, is still only faith compared with what shall come from that same Jesus in the glory of heaven.[7]

When God gives spiritual consolation, our response, Ignatius says, is to receive it, to be strengthened, enlightened, and encouraged by it.

Saint Francis of Assisi

Description of his time of conversion from an early Franciscan source:

He prayed unceasingly with tears and fasting, not relying on his own industry or virtue, but placing all his trust in God; and although he was still in the darkness of the world the Lord filled his soul with ineffable joy and a wonderful

[7] *Walter Hilton: The Scale of Perfection*, trans. John P. H. Clark and Rosemary Dorward (Paulist Press, 1991), 287–88.

light. Glowing with this inner radiance he left the cave, ready to face the insults and blows of his persecutors, and lightheartedly he took the road to Assisi. Trusting in Christ, his heart divinely aflame, Francis now reproached himself for his sloth and vain fears.[8]

Saint Pierre Favre

I took the solemn vows of my religious profession and sent them [in writing] to Master Iñigo [Ignatius], who had been elected superior general. As I made them I felt much spiritual consolation together with a great fortifying of my soul in the renunciation of the possessions I had already given up and the pleasures of the flesh I had already forsaken, and in humility, which consists in submission and in the denial of one's entire will. For all this, I say, I received fortitude anew and knowledge anew and deep feelings of goodwill.[9]

Again, the strengthening from receiving spiritual consolation, in this instance, to live his religious vows.

Saint John of Avila

Therefore, if the Lord gives someone consolations, let him accept them in order to carry his cross with greater strength, since the Lord's way is to console his disciples on Mount Tabor so that they may not be disturbed in the persecution of the cross. Ordinarily, before the gall of tribulation is presented, he sends the honey of consolation.[10]

[8] *Legend of the Three Companions*, in *St. Francis of Assisi*, ed. Habig, 907.

[9] *The Memoriale*, in *The Spiritual Writings of Pierre Favre*, trans. Edmond Murphy, S.J., and Martin Palmer, S.J. (Institute of Jesuit Sources, 1996), 77.

[10] *John of Avila: Audi, filia—Listen, O Daughter*, trans. Joan Francis Gormley (Paulist Press, 2006), 26, 98.

This is good counsel, that when you have fervor of spirit, reflect on how it will be when this light withdraws from you.[11]

Compare Ignatius' "Let one who is in consolation think how he will conduct himself in the desolation that will come after."

[11] *De Imitatione Christi*, bk. 3, chap. 7, author's translation. For complementary quotations, see Gallagher, *The Discernment of Spirits*: St. Elizabeth Seton (128–29); Timothy M. Gallagher, O.M.V., *Setting Captives Free: Personal Reflections on Ignatian Discernment of Spirits* (Crossroad, 2018): St. Ignatius (183), St. John of the Cross (184–85), St. Elizabeth Seton (185), St. Francis of Assisi (186).

Rule 11

Stay Humble During Consolation and Trust During Desolation

Rule 11 is the final rule in which Ignatius speaks of spiritual consolation and spiritual desolation.[1] It may be described as "the portrait of the mature person of discernment". All that Ignatius has said about consolation and desolation is directed toward this mature discernment. He writes:

> **Eleventh Rule.** Let one who is consoled seek to humble himself and lower himself as much as he can, thinking of how little he is capable in the time of desolation without such grace or consolation. On the contrary, let one who is in desolation think that he can do much with God's sufficient grace to resist all his enemies, taking strength in his Creator and Lord.

After a set of rules for one in desolation and a rule for one in consolation, Ignatius now brings the two together: "let one who is consoled" and "let one who is in desolation".

[1] Final rule in the First Set of rules; he addresses spiritual consolation in the Second Set as well.

Humble in Consolation

"Let one who is consoled seek to humble himself and lower himself as much as he can, thinking of how little he is capable in the time of desolation without such grace or consolation." Here Ignatius guards against a potential pitfall in time of spiritual consolation: With goodwill and energized by the consolation, these persons may imprudently overextend themselves, setting themselves up for a fall.

The man and the woman experience weeks of spiritual consolation. They find delight in prayer, in Mass and Eucharistic Adoration; they find joy in serving God in their vocations. Happy in this consolation, they now desire further spiritual growth. They wish to rise earlier and dedicate more time for prayer, volunteer for activities in the parish, make a retreat, and increase their spiritual reading. Yet Ignatius counsels, "Let one who is consoled seek to humble himself and lower himself as much as he can."

A salutary humility in time of spiritual consolation will defend them against such overconfidence and overextension. Ignatius urges this with a certain emphasis: "humble himself", "lower himself", "as much as he can".

Ever practical, Ignatius not only proposes such humility but also provides the way to acquire it. Once more, he calls us to *think* in a certain way—that is, "thinking of how little he is capable in the time of desolation without such grace or consolation". Ignatius advises that as the man and the woman live those weeks of consolation, they should call to mind and reflect on how little they can do, how they struggle, and how they incline to regress when they are in desolation, without the energizing grace of consolation. A truer perception of their strength will save them harmful overextension.

Trusting in Desolation

In the second part of this rule, Ignatius essentially summarizes what he has said thus far about our response to spiritual desolation: "On the contrary, let one who is in desolation think that he can do much with God's sufficient grace to resist all his enemies, taking strength in his Creator and Lord."

When the desolation presents the man or the woman to themselves as helpless, destined to succumb, Ignatius calls on them to *think* of the truth, that they can do *much*, that God's grace is *sufficient* to defeat *all* their spiritual enemies—all the lies, distortions, insinuations, and discouragements that they may face in desolation. Such thinking, such reflection, will lead them to take *new strength* in the Lord and help them to resist the desolation.

"Let one who is in desolation think that he can do much with God's sufficient grace to resist all his enemies." *All* his enemies. Ignatius used similar language in rule 2: "easing and taking away *all* obstacles". He likewise affirmed in rule 7 that "he can resist with the divine help, which *always* remains with him." Here, in rule 11, Ignatius once more repeats this surety: With God's sufficient grace, we can do much to resist *all* our spiritual enemies. His rules are a clarion call to confidence.

Neither naïvely and carelessly high in consolation, but wisely humble; nor blindly and hopelessly low in desolation, but confidently trusting—such is the portrait of the mature person of discernment.

Witnesses to Rule 11

Saint Francis de Sales

This is that holy evenness of mind which we should endeavor to possess; I do not say evenness of fancy, or of inclination, but of mind; for we need not make any account of the annoyances raised by the inferior part of our soul, whence all whims and inquietudes proceed, stirred up by the senses and passions, when the superior part of the soul does not perform its duty of being master, or when it does not keep good watch against the assaults and disturbances of its enemies, to make war upon them and subject them to its laws. I say that we must always remain firm and resolute in the superior part of our soul, for whose fidelity we make profession, and preserve a constant equanimity through favorable and unfavorable circumstances, in desolation as well as in consolation.[2]

Saint Ignatius of Loyola

In a letter dated June 18, 1536:

And so we must look carefully, and if the enemy lifts us up, we must lower ourselves, recounting our sins and miseries; if he lowers and depresses us, we must raise ourselves up with true faith and hope in the Lord, recalling the benefits received and with how much love and affection he waits to save us. The enemy does not care whether he speaks the truth or a lie, but only seeks to overcome us.[3]

Thomas à Kempis

When, therefore, spiritual consolation is given to you by God, receive it with gratitude and know that it is God's

[2] *The Consoling Thoughts of Saint Francis de Sales*, trans. Père Huguet (Aeterna Press, 2015), 56.

[3] *San Ignacio de Loyola: Obras* (Biblioteca de Autores Cristianos, 2013), 664, author's translation.

gift and not your merit, and so do not be lifted up with pride. Do not rejoice too much nor vainly presume because of it, but be more humble because of the gift and more watchful and fearful in all your actions, because this time will pass and temptation will follow.[4]

Saint Teresa of Avila

Since this edifice [the spiritual life] is built entirely on humility, the closer one comes to God the more progress there must be in this virtue.[5]

Once in comforting me He [the Lord] told me with much love that I shouldn't be anxious, that in this life we cannot always be in a stable condition, that sometimes the soul will experience fervor and at other times be without it, that sometimes it will have disturbances and at other times have quiet, and again temptations; but that it should hope in Him and not be afraid.[6]

Saint Thomas Aquinas

As stated above (I-II, Q. 23, A. 2) when we were treating of the passions, the difficult good has something attractive to the appetite, namely the aspect of good, and likewise something repulsive to the appetite, namely the difficulty

[4] *De Imitatione Christi*, bk. 2, chap. 9, author's translation.

[5] *The Book of Her Life*, in *The Collected Works of St. Teresa of Avila*, trans. Kieran Kavanaugh, O.C.D., and Otilio Rodriguez, O.C.D., vol. 1 (ICS Publications, 1976), 86–87.

[6] *Collected Works*, 1:282. These two quotations from St. Teresa of Avila are cited in Darío López Tejada, S.J., *Los ejercicios espirituales de San Ignacio de Loyola: Comentario y textos afines* (Edibesa, 1998), 877.

of obtaining it. In respect of the former there arises the movement of hope, and in respect of the latter, the movement of despair. Now it has been stated above (I-II, Q. 61, A. 2) that for those appetitive movements which are a kind of impulse towards an object, there is need of a moderating and restraining moral virtue, while for those which are a kind of recoil, there is need, on the part of the appetite, of a moral virtue to strengthen it and urge it on. Wherefore a twofold virtue is necessary with regard to the difficult good: one, to temper and restrain the mind, lest it tend to high things immoderately; and this belongs to the virtue of humility: and another to strengthen the mind against despair, and urge it on to the pursuit of great things according to right reason; and this is magnanimity. Therefore it is evident that humility is a virtue.[7]

A virtue is needed that will "temper and restrain the mind, lest it tend to high things immoderately; and this belongs to the virtue of humility."

Venerable Bruno Lanteri

Never let yourself be troubled, regardless of the state in which you find yourself, as, for example, when you feel that your faith is weak, when you find little interest in spiritual things, feel little movement of the heart in their regard, or when you experience resistance to these things, or any other defect or failing; but with simplicity of heart and humbling yourself before God, tell him with courage that you want to be his just as you are, and with even more defects than you recognize in yourself. Be sure that

[7] *Summa Theologica*, trans. Fathers of the English Dominican Province, vol. 4 (Christian Classics, 1981), II-II, q. 161, a. 1, co., p. 1842.

he came from heaven precisely for sinners [Lk 5:32] and that, according to his promise, he will pour out his help and grace abundantly where sin has been abundant [Rom 5:20]. To allow your heart to feel melancholy and discouragement is to follow the spirit of the tempter, because the Spirit of God leads us to confidence and peace.[8]

[8] *Pio Bruno Lanteri: Scritti e documenti d'archivio*, vol. 1 (Edizioni Lanteri, 2002), 747, author's translation. For complementary quotations, see Timothy M. Gallagher, O.M.V., *Setting Captives Free: Personal Reflections on Ignatian Discernment of Spirits* (Crossroad, 2018): St. Gregory the Great (199–200), Walter Hilton (200), Thomas à Kempis (200–201).

Rule 12

Stand Your Ground

In the final three rules, Ignatius addresses the other common tactic of the enemy: temptation. *Spiritual desolation* is a heavy movement of the heart on the spiritual level. *Temptation* is a deceptive suggestion of the enemy: "Why don't you let your prayer go until later? You can let yourself see that, have that, do that—it doesn't have to get too far out of hand."

Ignatius has already alerted us to the link between spiritual desolation and temptation (rules 4 and 7). He turns now specifically to this second tactic of the enemy. While the distinction between the two is real and should not be ignored, we need not overemphasize it either: In both cases, the same enemy is at work, with the same purpose, and, as we have seen, the two tactics may be found in combination.

In each of the three remaining rules, Ignatius highlights a quality of the enemy in his temptations so that, perceiving it, we will be prepared to reject it. In rules 12, 13, and 14, he expands the title of the enemy to the "the enemy of human nature", the one who is antihuman, opposed to human nature as God created it and desires it to be, with its destiny of eternal joy. Each rule comprises two parts: first a metaphor, a kind of symbolic parable, then its application to the enemy's corresponding tactic.

Rule 12 reads as follows:

> **Twelfth Rule.** The enemy acts as spoiled children do in being weak when faced with strength and strong when faced with weakness. For it is proper to spoiled children, when they begin to act out, to lose heart and desist when their parents confront them firmly; and, on the contrary, if their parents respond with weakness and helplessness, their acting out grows greatly and knows no bounds.[1] In the same way, it is proper to the enemy to weaken and lose heart, fleeing and ceasing his temptations when the person who is exercising himself in spiritual things confronts the temptations of the enemy firmly, doing what is diametrically opposed to them; and, on the contrary, if the person who is exercising himself begins to be afraid and lose heart in suffering the temptations, there is no beast so fierce on the face of the earth as the enemy of human nature in following out his damnable intention with such growing malice.

In his temptations, the enemy is "*weak* when faced *with strength* and *strong* when faced *with weakness*". This is the

[1] I have changed Ignatius' metaphor here to avoid distraction from the point he wishes to illustrate. David Fleming, S.J., adopts the metaphor of the spoiled child in *Draw Me into Your Friendship: A Literal Translation and a Contemporary Reading of the Spiritual Exercises* (Institute of Jesuit Sources, 1996), 257. Ignatius' original metaphor reads, "The enemy acts like a woman in being weak when faced with strength and strong when faced with weakness. For, as it is proper to a woman, when she is fighting with some man, to lose heart and to flee when the man confronts her firmly, and, on the contrary, if the man begins to flee, losing heart, the anger, vengeance and ferocity of the woman grow greatly and know no bounds." Obviously, such behavior is contrary to God's intention for men and women, as will be true of any metaphor of the action of "the enemy of human nature". In the spoiled-child metaphor, this antihuman quality is present—God does not intend children to be spoiled—but in a gentler way. For a discussion of this issue, see Timothy M. Gallagher, O.M.V., *The Discernment of Spirits: An Ignatian Guide for Everyday Living* (Crossroad, 2005), 150–52, including endnotes.

quality of the enemy's temptations that Ignatius wishes to highlight.

The spoiled child begins acting out. He pauses, looks at his parents, and sees that they are helpless, wringing their hands and supplicating. On he goes, and his bad behavior may exceed all bounds. Now let us consider a different scenario: The same child begins acting out. He pauses, looks at his parents, and sees that a loving but firm response will swiftly arrive. He desists in his acting out. The spoiled child can act out strongly only if his parents are weak in their response.

"In the same way," Ignatius says, "it is proper to the enemy to *weaken* and *lose heart*, *fleeing* and *ceasing his temptations*." When? "When the person who is exercising himself in spiritual things *confronts* the temptations of the enemy *firmly*, doing what is *diametrically opposed to them*".

The man spends time in Eucharistic Adoration on Saturday mornings and plans to do so this Saturday. But the preceding days have been difficult and desolate. He rises, prepares for the day, and feels no desire for Adoration. A thought comes: "Why don't you let it go until this afternoon? You should be able to go then." He responds, "No! I planned to do it this morning as usual, and I will not change my practice." He confronts the temptation of the enemy firmly, doing what is diametrically opposed to it—and the temptation is undone.

"On the contrary, if the person who is exercising himself begins to *be afraid and lose heart* in suffering the temptations, there is no beast *so fierce* on the face of the earth as the enemy of human nature in following out his damnable intention with such *growing* malice."

The same man spends time in Eucharistic Adoration on Saturday mornings and plans to do so this Saturday. But the preceding days have been difficult and desolate. He rises, prepares for the day, and feels no desire for Adoration. A thought comes: "Why don't you let it go until this afternoon? You should be able to go then." He responds, "Yes, maybe I could. I just don't feel like it now. I can do it later. Let me go online for a few minutes. Let me get some other things done." He has begun to be afraid and lose heart in facing the temptation; now it will strengthen and grow increasingly difficult to resist. The longer he delays, the less likely he is to spend time in Eucharistic Adoration this Saturday.

There is a snowball effect to the enemy's temptations. Here is a high mountain peak, covered in snow. At the peak, a snowball is just getting started. You can put out a finger and stop it. But let it get halfway down the mountainside, gaining mass and speed, and it will run you over.[2]

When, therefore, is it easiest to resist the enemy's temptations? *Right in the very beginning.* When you stop the snowball at the top of the mountain, you never have to deal with an avalanche later.

When is it easiest to resist the temptation to use the smartphone in a "low and earthly" way? *Before you even touch the screen.* One touch, fifty touches, one hundred touches later, the temptation grows increasingly hard to resist. The same is true of the enemy's temptations in general. Rule 12, if we practice it, saves us much suffering in the spiritual life.

Jesus, the Friend of Human Nature

Note the vocabulary Ignatius uses with regard to the enemy. Do we ever think of the enemy as "weakening"? As "losing heart"? As "fleeing"? As "ceasing his temptations"? Ignatius wants to undo the enemy's false self-presentation as all-powerful. The enemy is not weak compared to us, but he is utterly weak compared to Christ and the power of his

[2] Gallagher, *The Discernment of Spirits*, 153.

grace in us (Lk 11:21–22). If, with God's grace, we are willing to "confront the temptations of the enemy firmly, doing what is diametrically opposed to them", the enemy's weakness is revealed: He loses heart, flees, ceases his temptations.

The evil one is "the enemy of human nature". Pope Francis writes that Jesus is " 'the friend of human nature,' ... who wants to win us for God and to recapitulate in himself all that is good in creation, in order to offer it to the Father, to the praise of his glory".[3] What a lovely way to understand Jesus.

Witnesses to Rule 12

Saint Thomas Aquinas

Speaking of the temptations that Christ willed to undergo and how the enemy acts in his temptations:

The temptation which comes from the enemy takes the form of a suggestion, as Gregory says (*Hom.* xvi, *in Evang.*). Now a suggestion cannot be made to everybody in the same way; it must arise from those things towards which each one has an inclination. Consequently the devil does not straight away tempt the spiritual man to grave sins, but he begins with lighter sins, so as gradually to lead him to those of greater magnitude. Wherefore Gregory (*Moral.* xxxi), expounding Job 39:25, "He smells the battle from afar, the encouraging of the captains and the shouting of the army," says: "The captains are fittingly described as encouraging, and the army as shouting. Because vices begin by insinuating themselves into the mind under some specious pretext:

[3] *In Him Alone Is Our Hope: Spiritual Exercises Given to His Brother Bishops in the Manner of Saint Ignatius of Loyola* (Magnificat, 2013), 69.

then they come on the mind in such numbers as to drag it into all sorts of folly, deafening it with their bestial clamor."

Thus, too, did the devil set about the temptation of the first man. For at first he enticed his mind to consent to the eating of the forbidden fruit, saying (Gen 3:1): "Why has God commanded you that you should not eat of every tree of paradise?" Secondly [he tempted him] to vainglory by saying: "Your eyes shall be opened." Thirdly, he led the temptation to the extreme height of pride, saying: "You shall be as gods, knowing good and evil." This same order did he observe in tempting Christ. For at first he tempted Him to that which men desire, however spiritual they may be—namely, the support of the corporeal nature by food. Secondly, he advanced to that matter in which spiritual men are sometimes found wanting, inasmuch as they do certain things for show, which pertains to vainglory. Thirdly, he led the temptation on to that in which no spiritual men, but only carnal men, have a part—namely, to desire worldly riches and fame, to the extent of holding God in contempt. And so in the first two temptations he said: "If You be the Son of God"; but not in the third, which is inapplicable to spiritual men, who are sons of God by adoption, whereas it does apply to the two preceding temptations.

And Christ resisted these temptations by quoting the authority of the Law, not by enforcing His power, "so as to give more honor to His human nature and a greater punishment to His adversary, since the foe of the human race was vanquished, not as by God, but as by man," as Pope Leo says (*Serm.* 1, *De Quadrag.* 3).[4]

Temptation is easiest to resist in its very beginning, before it grows stronger.

[4] *Summa Theologica*, trans. Fathers of the English Dominican Province, vol. 4 (Christian Classics, 1981), III, q. 42, a. 4, co., p. 2238, brackets in original. As above, I have lightly adapted the biblical quotations in accord with more contemporary usage.

Jesus decisively rejects all these temptations and reiterates his firm resolve to follow the path set by the Father, without any kind of compromise with sin or worldly logic. Note well how Jesus responds. He does not dialogue with Satan, as Eve had done in the earthly paradise. Jesus is well aware that there can be no dialogue with Satan, for he is cunning. That is why Jesus, instead of engaging in dialogue as Eve had, chooses to take refuge in the Word of God and responds with the power of this Word. Let us remember this: at the moment of temptation, of our temptations, there is no arguing with Satan, our defence must always be the Word of God! And this will save us.[5]

Look around us—it is enough to open a newspaper, as I said—we see the presence of evil, the devil is acting. However, I would like to say out loud: God is stronger! Do you believe this, that God is stronger? Let us say it together, let us say it all together: God is stronger! And do you know why he is stronger? Because He is Lord, the only Lord.[6]

Saint Augustine

Listen carefully, make sure you understand, and take warning: *She will watch for your head, and you for her heel* [Gen 3:15]. Watch closely, O Church, for the snake's head. What is the snake's head? The first suggestion of sin. Some

[5] Angelus (March 9, 2014), https://www.vatican.va/content/francesco/en/angelus/2014/documents/papa-francesco_angelus_20140309.html.

[6] General Audience (June 12, 2013), https://www.vatican.va/content/francesco/en/audiences/2013/documents/papa-francesco_20130612_udienza-generale.html.

unlawful thought enters your mind. Do not dwell on it, do not consent to it. What came into your mind was the snake's head: trample on it, and you will be safe from any more of his movements. What does this mean, to trample on his head? Repudiate the suggestion.[7]

The head of the serpent: another metaphor for the same teaching.

Adolphe Tanqueray, P.S.S.

On how to respond to temptations:

Promptly, without parleying with the enemy, without any hesitation. At the outset the temptation is repelled easily enough, for it has not yet gained a foothold in the soul; if we wait until it has gained entry, the repulse will prove far more difficult. Hence, let there be no debate.[8]

Thomas à Kempis

As a man has said, take remedy for the illness in its beginning, or the medicine will be applied too late. For first a simple thought comes to the mind, then a strong imagination, then pleasure in it, and evil stirrings, and finally consent. Thus, the enemy, little by little, gains full entrance because he was not resisted in the beginning. And the slower one is in resisting, the weaker he grows daily and the enemy stronger against him....

[7] "Exposition 4 of Psalm 103", in *The Works of Saint Augustine: Expositions of the Psalms*, ed. Boniface Ramsey, trans. Maria Boulding, O.S.B., vol. 19 (New City Press, 2003), 172, italics in original.

[8] *The Spiritual Life: A Treatise on Ascetical and Mystical Theology* (TAN Books, 2000), 434, italics in original.

Therefore, we should not despair when we are tempted but pray to God the more fervently that he indeed deign to help us in every tribulation, according to the words of Saint Paul, that in time of temptation he grant us grace that we may bear it [1 Cor 10:13]. Let us humble ourselves, therefore, under the hand of God in every temptation and trial, because the humble of heart will be saved and rejoice.[9]

"Resisted in the beginning".

Saint Teresa of Calcutta

If we allow ourselves to be unfaithful in little things and say, "It doesn't matter," the day will come when we want to get rid of it, and we will be so blinded that we won't know how to. Jesus tells us this in one word when he describes the devil as the father of lies. He even came to Jesus as an angel of light to tempt him in the wilderness. First he told him, "You are hungry and that is a very good reason to turn stone into bread!" But, if Jesus had done that, he would have been placing material things above the will of God. "My food is to do the will of the one who sent me" [Jn 4:34]. And what did Jesus answer him? "Man does not live on bread alone but on every word that comes from the mouth of God" [Mt 4:4]. Even a stupid man would say that Jesus had the right to change stones into bread. He had been fasting for forty days, and nobody could possibly object or complain about it. Maybe if Jesus had given in, the devil would have tempted him a little more. When he was hanging on the Cross and they were jeering at him to "Come down from the Cross for you are in great pain"

[9] *De Imitatione Christi*, bk. 1, chap. 13, author's translation.

[Mt 27:40], he might have come down if he had said "yes" the first time.[10]

Saint Ignatius of Loyola

During the months at Manresa after his conversion:

There occurred to him a rather disturbing thought which troubled him by representing to him the difficulty of the life he was leading, as though he heard a voice within him saying: "How can you stand a life like this for the seventy years you have yet to live?" But this he answered also interiorly with great strength, feeling that it was the voice of the enemy: "You poor creature! Can you promise me even one hour of life?" In this way he overcame the temptation and remained at peace.[11]

The response is immediate and diametrically opposed to the temptation, which is thereby overcome.

Saint Pierre Favre

On Good Friday, while hearing the confessions of the children of a certain nobleman, one of my spiritual sons, certain proud thoughts came to mind as well as the spirit that put certain questions to me such as these: Did you come here to spend your energies on these youngsters? Would it not be more profitable to be where you could hear the confessions of the grown-ups? I resolved then and

[10] *Mother Teresa: Where There Is Love, There Is God*, ed. Brian Kolodiejchuk, M.C. (Doubleday, 2010), 109.

[11] *St. Ignatius' Own Story: As Told to Luis Gonzalez de Camara*, trans. William J. Young, S.J. (Loyola University Press, 1980), 18.

there, if God should so will it, to spend my entire life on nothing else except on such works as these which in themselves seem to be so lowly and insignificant. Great consolation, born of the spirit of humility, followed on this resolve, and my eyes were opened to see, as I never saw before, the value of work done with a right intention for God's little ones.[12]

"I resolved then and there."

Saint Francis de Sales

As soon as you are conscious of being tempted, follow the example of children when they see a wolf or bear out in the country. They immediately run to the arms of their father or mother or at least call to them for help and protection. Turn in the same way to God and implore his mercy and help. This is the remedy our Lord himself has taught us: "Pray that you do not enter into temptation [Mt 26:41]."...

Never argue with your enemy or answer him with any words but those of our Savior when he put him to rout: "Begone, Satan, 'the Lord your God shall you adore and him only shall you serve!'" [Mt 4:10]. A chaste wife must never answer a single word to the base wretch that makes her a dishonorable proposal, nor should she look him in the face. Without any discussion she must leave him abruptly and at the same instant turn her heart toward her husband and renew the fidelity she has promised him. So also when a devout soul sees itself attacked by temptation, it must not lose time in argument or discussion but with

[12] Quoted in William V. Bangert, S.J., *To the Other Towns: A Life of Blessed Peter Favre, First Companion of Saint Ignatius* (Ignatius Press, 2002), 267.

all simplicity turn toward Jesus Christ, its spouse, and affirm again its fidelity to him and its desire to be solely and entirely his forever.[13]

"Immediately". "Never argue". "Never answer". "Without any discussion".

J. R. R. Tolkien

On how Gollum might have avoided the temptation of the Ring:

Need it ever have crossed his path? Need anything dangerous ever cross any of our paths? A kind of answer [could] be found in trying to imagine Gollum overcoming temptation. The story would have been quite different! By temporizing, not fixing the still not wholly corrupt Sméagol-will towards good in the debate in the slag hole, he weakened himself for the final chance when dawning love of Frodo was too easily withered by the jealousy of Sam before Shelob's lair. After that he was lost.[14]

The "temporizing" with temptation that allows it to grow stronger.

[13] *Introduction to the Devout Life*, trans. John K. Ryan (Image Books, 1950), 233–35.

[14] *The Letters of J. R. R Tolkien*, ed. Humphrey Carpenter and Christopher Tolkien (Houghton Mifflin, 1981), 235. See also J. R. R. Tolkien, "The Passage of the Marshes", bk. 4, chap. 2 in *The Two Towers* (Ballantine Books, 1965). For complementary quotations, see Gallagher, *The Discernment of Spirits*: St. Ignatius (154–55, 157), St. Francis of Assisi (157–58); Timothy M. Gallagher, O.M.V., *Setting Captives Free: Personal Reflections on Ignatian Discernment of Spirits* (Crossroad, 2018): St. Anthony of the Desert (209), St. Thomas More (209), St. Teresa of Avila (210), Venerable Bruno Lanteri (210), Thomas à Kempis (211–12, 213–14), Evagrius (213), St. Benedict (213), St. Ignatius (214), St. Alphonsus de Liguori (214), St. Thérèse of Lisieux (214–15).

Rule 13

Speak with a Competent Person

In discussing rule 5, we said that this rule would guide us safely through almost any spiritual darkness: Never change your spiritual proposals in time of spiritual desolation. Now we can complete that statement. Rules 5 and 13, if we practice them together, will guide us safely through any spiritual darkness we may ever encounter: Do not change your spiritual proposals in time of desolation (rule 5) and speak about the burden with a wise and competent spiritual person (rule 13).

Rule 13 reads:

> Thirteenth Rule. Likewise he conducts himself as a false lover in wishing to remain secret and not be revealed. For a dissolute man who, speaking with evil intention, makes dishonorable advances to a daughter of a good father or a wife of a good husband, wishes his words and persuasions to be secret, and the contrary displeases him very much, when the daughter reveals to her father or the wife to her husband his false words and depraved intention, because he easily perceives that he will not be able to succeed with the undertaking begun. In the same way, when the enemy of human nature brings his wiles and persuasions to the just soul, he wishes and desires that they be received and kept in secret; but when one reveals them to one's good confessor or to another spiritual person, who knows his deceits and malicious designs, it weighs on him very

> much, because he perceives that he will not be able to succeed with the malicious undertaking he has begun, since his manifest deceits have been revealed.

Ignatius presents the enemy as a "false lover"—that is, one who does not seek the good of the beloved but rather seeks to seduce and use the other for his selfish purpose. The false lover wishes "to *remain secret* and *not be revealed*". This is the quality of the enemy that Ignatius highlights: He desires that his temptations, his discouraging lies, his burdens remain secret, that the one tempted not reveal them to a competent spiritual person.

The metaphor is clear. When the false lover makes dishonorable advances to the daughter or wife, "he wishes that his words and persuasions" remain secret, that she not speak of this to her father or husband. He knows that as long as she does not, his "game" can go on. He also knows that *in the moment itself* when the daughter speaks of this to her father or the wife to her husband, he will be utterly defeated. When they do speak, Ignatius writes, this "displeases him very much,... because he easily perceives that he will not be able to succeed with the undertaking begun". Thus, he urges the daughter or wife, "Don't say anything about this. You can't speak about this. Keep this to yourself."

Ignatius then applies the metaphor: "In the same way," when the enemy brings his "wiles and persuasions" to the "just soul"—to anyone sincerely seeking to live the Christian life—he wishes us to keep silent about them: temptations, doubts, fears, burdens, discouraging lies, anxieties, and anything else that weighs on our freedom to be loved by and to love the Lord.

Here, more than in all that has preceded, great reverence and sensitivity are needed. Rule 13 may touch deep places in our hearts.

The Burden

This may be something from the past or something occurring now in our lives about which we have never said anything to anyone, but it weighs upon our relationship with the Lord. In our hearts, we say, "I would feel so free, Lord, to receive your love and to love you in return, were it not for ..." And there it is, the burden. Then the enemy urges, "You can't talk about this—don't say anything about this", because as long as we do not, the game can go on. The enemy wishes, Ignatius writes, that these spiritual burdens be "received [when they first arise] and kept [over the course of days, weeks, months, years] in secret".

If this is the enemy's tactic, what is to be our response? Ignatius writes, "When one *reveals* them to one's good confessor or to another spiritual person, who knows his deceits and malicious designs, it weighs on him very much, because he perceives that he will not be able to succeed with the malicious undertaking he has begun, since his manifest deceits have been *revealed*." Our response is to *break the spiritual silence*, to *reveal* these burdens to the proper spiritual person. This, Ignatius says, weighs on the enemy "very much" because he knows that *the act itself* of speaking openly with a competent spiritual person will bring freedom from his burdens.

The Person

Ignatius specifies that we do not speak with just anyone. With economy of words, he outlines two profiles of the person with whom we may speak: "one's good confessor or ... another spiritual person, who knows [the enemy's] deceits and malicious designs".

First, he recommends speaking to "one's good confessor". This is a priest, and one with whom we have had contact in the Sacrament of Confession. But it is not just any confessor; it is a *good* confessor. "Good", as Ignatius immediately clarifies, does not mean simply devout—a wonderful quality in a confessor—but *knowledgeable.* This is a confessor who knows the enemy's "deceits and malicious designs", so that when we share our burden, he will understand and be prepared to help us. "One's" good confessor indicates that we know this priest to be such a confessor through personal experience of him.

Second, Ignatius recommends speaking to "another spiritual person". This could be a person in any vocation: priest, religious, or lay. Again, not just any person, but a *spiritual* person—that is, not only devout but also *knowledgeable*, "who knows [the enemy's] deceits and malicious designs". Because this spiritual person is knowledgeable, he will be competent to understand and help. Very likely, this will be a person with formal training in spiritual direction.

The Imagined Scenario

The enemy's incitement to secrecy operates through an imagined scenario. "If you speak about this with the confessor or spiritual person, it will be awkward, humiliating, useless—it will just make things worse. It is better, therefore, to say nothing." This imagined scenario may take different forms.[1]

[1] See Timothy M. Gallagher, O.M.V., *Setting Captives Free: Personal Reflections on Ignatian Discernment of Spirits* (Crossroad, 2018), 225–27.

"I could speak with him, but he is too busy."

In the short term, depending on how busy this person is at the moment, this may be true. But if weeks pass and you still hesitate for this reason, you need to think in terms of rule 13: There is an enemy who does not want you to speak. Let the person you need to speak with take responsibility for his time; you need not take this upon yourself. If he is too busy, he will tell you. But do not hesitate to ask. You only honor such a person when you do.

"I could speak with him, but I am too busy."

Again, in the short term and depending on how busy you are at the moment, this may be true. But if weeks pass and you are still "too busy" to speak with this person, you need to remember the enemy who does not want you to speak. You are not too busy to meet with this person.

"If I talk about this, he will laugh at me."

This may be the most painful imagined scenario of all. Absolutely not! If this is the wise and competent spiritual person Ignatius intends, his esteem for you will grow as you share. He will appreciate the courage this required and love the desire for growth that led you to speak.

"If I talk about this, he will never understand me."

Again, if this is the wise and competent person Ignatius describes, the opposite will be true. In all likelihood, this person will understand the situation better than you, both because of his training and because of greater objectivity. The experience of centuries in the Church confirms this truth.

"If I talk about this, he will be kind but will never respect me again in the same way."

Again, absolutely not! This person will admire the courage your sharing required and honor your desire to grow. His respect for you will increase.

"If I talk about this, he will end our work together."

The same comment as the preceding. This person will be happier to work with you because now the conversation can focus on the real need and so prove more fruitful.

"Why talk about it? Nothing anyone can say will change it."

Experience consistently refutes this. And even were the person to have little to say, the act itself of speaking about the burden with this person will do much to free you from it. Do not believe this lie of the enemy.

Forms of Spiritual Accompaniment

Ignatius never conceives of the discerning life as lived in isolation. Spiritual accompaniment, which may take various forms, is always a part of this life. I believe that, in the long run, perseverance in the discerning life or failure to persevere depends upon whether we are alone or accompanied.

If this is perennially true, it is the more urgent today in a culture that increasingly challenges our faith. Pope Benedict XVI affirms, "To advance toward the Lord, we always have need of a guide, of some form of dialogue; we cannot do it just with our own reflections."[2] We all have need of some form of dialogue. An overview of such forms follows. Ideally, each of us will adopt a mixture of these forms.

Spiritual Direction

Where this is possible, spiritual direction is a classic and proven form of accompaniment. In normal circumstances, director and directee meet monthly for about an hour. The focus is the directee's relationship with God. The director listens, helps the directee see more clearly where God might be leading, and likewise assists in identifying tactics of the enemy. This is an age-old and proven form of accompaniment in the Church.

Confession

For some, finding a spiritual director may be difficult, but all have access to the Sacrament of Confession. We may note that a confessor is one of the profiles Ignatius mentions as a person with whom we may speak. Regular Confession, if possible with a priest we find especially helpful, can be an invaluable form of spiritual dialogue. The sharing may of necessity be brief, but regular spiritual sharing of this kind is a powerful means to defeat the enemy's push to secrecy.

[2] General Audience (September 16, 2009), https://www.vatican.va/content/benedict-xvi/en/audiences/2009/documents/hf_ben-xvi_aud_20090916.html.

Retreats

An annual retreat, most likely a weekend, is a time-honored and classic practice in our spiritual tradition. Often, such retreats include the option of speaking privately with the retreat director. Great blessings for the entire year may flow from such conversations.

Spiritual Friends

Friends with whom one can share the spiritual life help greatly. This is not spiritual direction, in which one person serves another, but a relationship of mutuality, friends who support each other on the spiritual journey. Today, with phone and video options added to in-person conversation, the possibilities are wide. Do you know anyone with whom you could share in this way?

Spiritual Groups

These may be parish groups, chapters of spiritual associations, or groups created locally. They may be in person or virtual. Belonging to a spiritual community provides great encouragement on the journey of faith.

Married Couples

Where possible—and the effort to attain this is eminently worthwhile—husbands and wives find their closest form of spiritual accompaniment in the home and at the heart of their married vocation. Such accompaniment exists only in the married vocation and is a great blessing of this vocation. Neither husband nor wife seeks to be the spiritual director of the other but rather a friend with whom to pray and speak about spiritual matters.[3]

Family

In their special way, family members may accompany one another on the spiritual journey. A shared life of the sacraments, prayer, and conversation together about the life of faith are enormously beneficial—a beautiful "form of dialogue" for mutual inspiration.

As mentioned previously, ideally each of us is accompanied in several of these ways. These are likely the most effective steps we can take toward living the discerning life. None of us is meant to live faith alone; rather, we are called to community.

Witnesses to Rule 13

Saint Catherine of Siena

When [evil] thoughts or strong temptations regarding some specific thing (no matter how ugly) come into your heart, never keep them inside, but reveal them to the father of our soul. For the devil very much likes it when we hold on to these things and doesn't like it at all when we tell them. Why? When we hold on to them we become confused; then we get discouraged and give up our spiritual

[3] See Timothy Gallagher, O.M.V., *Discernment of Spirits in Marriage: Ignatian Wisdom for Husbands and Wives* (Sophia Institute Press, 2020).

exercises. This often leads to despair—just what the devil wants. So we mustn't be afraid, but must reveal our every infirmity to the doctor of our souls, with hope in Christ's blood.[4]

Saint Teresa of Avila

The safest thing, as the Lord told me, is to make known to my confessor the whole state of my soul and the favors God grants me, that he be learned, and that I obey him. The Lord has often told me this. It is what I do, and without doing so I would have no peace.[5]

Saint John of the Cross

Whoever wants to stand alone without the support of a master and guide will be like the tree that stands alone in a field without a proprietor. No matter how much the tree bears, passers-by will pick the fruit before it ripens.

A tree that is cultivated and guarded through the care of its owner produces its fruit at the expected time.

The virtuous soul that is alone and without a master is like a lone burning coal; it will grow colder rather than hotter.

Those who fall alone remain alone in their fall, and they value their soul little since they entrust it to themselves alone.

[4] *The Letters of Catherine of Siena*, trans. Suzanne Noffke, O.P., vol. 2 (Arizona Center for Medieval and Renaissance Studies, 2001), 650–51.

[5] *The Book of Her Life*, in *The Collected Works of St. Teresa of Avila*, trans. Kieran Kavanaugh, O.C.D., and Otilio Rodriguez, O.C.D., vol. 1 (ICS Publications, 1976), 171.

If you do not fear falling alone, do you presume that you will rise up alone? Consider how much more can be accomplished by two together than by one alone.[6]

Saint Francis of Assisi

Speaking with the two elders when seeking Lady Poverty, an allegory of the origins of the Franciscans:

Take with you some faithful companions that you may listen to their advice as you go up the mountain and be strengthened by their help, for woe to the solitary man! For if he should fall, he has no one to lift him up [Eccles 4:10].[7]

Saint Francis de Sales

The sovereign remedy against all temptation, whether great or small, is to open your heart and express its suggestions, feelings, and affections to your director. Note well that the first condition the evil one makes with a soul he desires to seduce is for it to keep silence, just as those who want to seduce girls or women from the very first forbid them to say anything about their proposals to father or husband. On the other hand, in his inspirations God

[6] *The Sayings of Light and Love*, in *The Collected Works of St. John of the Cross*, 3rd ed., trans. Kieran Kavanaugh, O.C.D., and Otilio Rodriguez, O.C.D. (ICS Publications, 1991), 86.

[7] *Sacrum Commercium*, 11, in *St. Francis of Assisi: Writings and Early Biographies; English Omnibus of the Sources for the Life of St. Francis*, ed. Marion A. Habig (Franciscan Herald Press, 1973), 1556.

requires that we make the temptations known to our superiors and directors.[8]

There are various remedies to temptation; one is sovereign.

One of the safest remedies is to [open] our heart, without concealing anything, to some prudent and spiritual person, mentioning to him the resentments, attachments, and suggestions that proceed from our sadness, and the reasons with which we entertain them; and all this humbly and faithfully. The first condition that the devil imposes on a soul which he wishes to afflict and seduce, is silence, just as the seditious do in conspiracies, for they require above all things that their undertakings and resolutions should be kept secret. God, on the contrary, requires discretion as the first condition; not wishing indeed that we should indiscreetly discover His graces and favors, but that we should make them known with prudence, and according to the rules of an humble discretion, to persons endowed with the requisite qualities.[9]

"One of the safest remedies."

Resolve to accept willingly all the inspirations it may please God to send you.... But before you consent to inspirations with regard to important or extraordinary things, always consult your adviser so that he may examine the inspiration and see whether it is true or false. When the enemy sees a soul ready to consent to inspirations he often proposes false ones in order to deceive it. He can never accomplish this as long as that soul humbly obeys its director.[10]

[8] *Introduction to the Devout Life*, trans. John K. Ryan (Image Books, 1950), 234.

[9] *The Consoling Thoughts of Saint Francis de Sales*, trans. Père Huguet (Aeterna Press, 2015), 98. I have changed the verb "discover" in the translation to "open" for greater clarity.

[10] *Introduction to the Devout Life*, 100.

Saint Thérèse of Lisieux

Of her Confession to Father Alexis Prou, O.F.M. Rec., retreat director:

At the time I was having great interior trials of all kinds, even to the point of asking myself whether heaven really existed. I felt disposed to say nothing of my interior dispositions since I didn't know how to express them, but I had hardly entered the confessional when I felt my soul expand. After speaking only a few words, *I was understood* in a marvelous way and my soul was like a book in which this priest read better than I did myself. He launched me full sail upon the waves of *confidence and love* which so strongly attracted me, but upon which I dared not advance. He told me that *my faults caused God no pain, and that holding as he did God's place*, he was telling me *in His name* that God was very much pleased with me.

Oh! how happy I was to hear those consoling words! Never had I heard that our faults *could not cause God any pain*, and this assurance filled me with joy, helping me to bear patiently with life's exile. I felt at the bottom of my heart that this was really so, for God is more tender than a mother.[11]

Catechism of the Catholic Church

The regular confession of our venial sins helps us form our conscience, fight against evil tendencies, let ourselves be

[11] *Story of a Soul: The Autobiography of St. Thérèse of Lisieux*, 3rd ed., trans. John Clarke, O.C.D. (ICS Publications, 1996), 173–74, italics in original.

healed by Christ and progress in the life of the Spirit. By receiving more frequently through this sacrament the gift of the Father's mercy, we are spurred to be merciful as he is merciful.[12]

Pope Francis

God's voice and that of the tempter, speak in different "environments": the enemy prefers darkness, falsehood, and gossip; the Lord loves sunlight, truth, and sincere transparency. The enemy will say to us: "Close yourself up in yourself, besides no one understands and listens to you, do not be trusting!" Goodness, on the contrary, invites us to open up, to be clear and trusting in God and in others.[13]

In a letter to priests:

I would encourage you not to neglect spiritual direction. Look for a brother with whom you can speak, reflect, discuss and discern, sharing with complete trust and openness your journey. A wise brother with whom to share the experience of discipleship. Find him, meet with him and enjoy his guidance, accompaniment and counsel. This is an indispensable aid to carrying out your ministry in obedience to the will of the Father (cf. *Heb* 10:9) and letting your heart beat with "the mind that was in Christ Jesus" (*Phil* 2:5). We can profit from the words of Ecclesiastes: "Two are better than one.... One will lift up the other;

[12] *Catechism of the Catholic Church*, no. 1458; cf. Lk 6:36.

[13] Regina Caeli (May 3, 2020), https://www.vatican.va/content/francesco/en/angelus/2020/documents/papa-francesco_regina-coeli_20200503.html.

but woe to the one who is alone and falls, and does not have another to help!" (4:9–10).[14]

"This is an indispensable aid to carrying out your ministry." Indispensable: "absolutely necessary, not subject to being set aside or neglected".[15]

Walter Hilton (Fourteenth-Century English Augustinian Writer)

Counseling those undergoing temptations:

It is good for them to open their minds to some wise man in the beginning, before these temptations get rooted in their heart, and that they forsake their own wit and judgement and follow the counsel of another. But that they show them not unadvisedly or lightly to any unskillful or worldly man, who never felt such temptations, for such may easily by their unskillfulness bring a simple soul into despair.[16]

Bring the temptation to a wise and competent spiritual person (rule 13), "in the beginning" (rule 12).

[14] Letter of His Holiness Pope Francis to Priests (August 4, 2019), https://www.vatican.va/content/francesco/en/letters/2019/documents/papa-francesco_20190804_lettera-presbiteri.html.

[15] *Merriam-Webster Dictionary*, "indispensable", accessed December 11, 2025, https://www.merriam-webster.com/dictionary/indispensable.

[16] *The Scale (or Ladder) of Perfection*, chap. 2, https://www.ccel.org/ccel/h/hilton/ladder/cache/ladder.pdf. For complementary quotations, see Timothy M. Gallagher, O.M.V., *The Discernment of Spirits: An Ignatian Guide for Everyday Living* (Crossroad, 2005): St. Thérèse of Lisieux (164–68), Thomas Merton (168–71); Gallagher, *Setting Captives Free*: Benedict XVI (227–28).

Rule 14

Strengthen the Stronghold

One issue remains. We may find ourselves saying, at this point, "Saint Ignatius, all this is helpful, and I can see how it will bless me in my spiritual life. But it is hard to believe that this one area can ever change." In rule 14, Ignatius turns to that place where we feel most helpless, where we hope least for change, for freedom. He will not conclude his rules without addressing this vulnerable place with sensitivity and reverence, without bringing light and hope to it. We might title rule 14 "Hope where we feel least hopeful". In this final rule, Ignatius traces a path to freedom even there.

As in the preceding two rules, Ignatius presents a metaphor, which he then applies to the spiritual life:

> **Fourteenth Rule.** Likewise he conducts himself as a leader, intent upon conquering and robbing what he desires. For, just as a captain and leader of an army in the field, pitching his camp and exploring the fortifications and defenses of a stronghold, attacks it at the weakest point, in the same way the enemy of human nature, roving about, looks in turn at all our theological, cardinal, and moral virtues; and where he finds us weakest and most in need for our eternal salvation, there he attacks us and attempts to take us.

The enemy is pictured as the astute leader of a group of brigands and thieves, "intent upon conquering and robbing what he desires". As the townspeople watch from behind the walls of their castle, they see the brigands arrive and set up camp on the plain below. As they look, the leader, accompanied by his lieutenants, slowly rides the circuit of the walls. They see him study the approach of the land, the thickness and repair of the walls, the towers, and the gates. The moment comes when the leader identifies the weakest point in the defenses of the castle. A less-skilled eye might not perceive it, but he sees it clearly. Shortly thereafter, the attack begins at that weakest point.

Ignatius now applies the metaphor. "In the same way", he writes, "the enemy of human nature, roving about, looks in turn at all our theological, cardinal, and moral virtues,"—that is to say, at the whole of our spiritual lives: our prayer, our acts of service, the living of our vocation, our relationships, what gives us strength, what discourages us, and what causes us to fear. "And *where* he finds us weakest and most in need for our eternal salvation, *there* he attacks us and attempts to take us."

We all have some point where we are most vulnerable to the enemy's discouraging lies and temptations. There is no shame in this. From our physical humanity, our individual temperaments, our family upbringing, our emotional dynamics, and our life experiences—from living in a fallen, redeemed, and loved world—arises some aspect of our spiritual lives in which our spiritual defenses are weakest. *There*, Ignatius says, the enemy "attacks us and attempts to take us".

If this is the enemy's tactic, what is to be our response?

On a day of peace, the townspeople gather and say, "From time to time, we are attacked by roving bands of thieves. We would do well to examine our defenses to ensure their strength and readiness for attack." The leader of the town, accompanied by his assistants, rides out the gate of the castle. He slowly makes the circuit of the walls. He studies the approach of the land, the thickness and repair of the walls, the towers, and the gates. The moment comes when he perceives the weakest point in the defenses of the castle.

The townspeople set to work. They strip away the crumbling masonry and replace it with solid blocks of stone. They increase the thickness of the wall and raise it higher.

Now a day comes when they see the brigands set up camp below, see the leader approach and ride the circuit of the castle, see him study the thickness and repair of the walls, the towers, and the gates. But this time things are different. The weak point is no longer weak. Now the enemy has only two choices: to attack at that point, but now in the face of strong defenses, or to attack at another place in the walls, again faced with strong defenses. His task is much harder and his victory much less certain.

This is the final place of spiritual freedom to which Ignatius calls us in his fourteen rules: to know, even before the enemy tempts and disquiets, where the attack will come and to prepare strong spiritual defenses in advance of that attack.

Identifying the Vulnerable Point

Self-knowledge is the key. Centuries ago, Saint Augustine prayed, "Domine Jesu, noverim me, noverim te" (Lord Jesus, may I know myself, and may I know you).[1]

Understood in its Christian truth, self-knowledge is the source of the greatest happiness in our lives. Who am I? I am a beloved son, a beloved daughter of the Heavenly

[1] *Soliloquies* 2, 1, 1.

Father, loved infinitely from all eternity, created out of love, redeemed with infinite love, and called to an eternity of joy. This is our deepest identity. Because we wish to live that identity, we desire to know where it is most threatened, in order to defend against the threat. Such is the invitation of rule 14.

Reflection on the following questions may help identify that point of vulnerability in your own life:[2]

- Is there some situation that frequently discourages me in my spiritual life or that strips me of spiritual energy?
- Are there circumstances in my spiritual life in which I often become afraid or in which I feel spiritually helpless?
- Is there one recurring way in which I find myself spiritually weakened?
- Is there something that habitually disheartens me in prayer or that causes me to doubt God's love for me?
- Is there a *repeating pattern* of these experiences?

The answers to these questions will likely reveal the vulnerable point in your life. Once it is perceived, you can begin to strengthen it, with blessed consequences in your spiritual life.

Strengthening the Vulnerable Point

How might we do this? Our spiritual tradition offers us effective answers to this question.[3]

[2] See Timothy M. Gallagher, O.M.V., *The Discernment of Spirits: An Ignatian Guide for Everyday Living* (Crossroad, 2005), 182, and Timothy M. Gallagher, O.M.V., *Setting Captives Free: Personal Reflections on Ignatian Discernment of Spirits* (Crossroad, 2018), 245–46.

[3] See Gallagher, *Setting Captives Free*, 247–51.

Prayer

"Ask, and it will be given to you.... For every one who asks receives" (Mt 7:7–8). Prayer is the first means toward strengthening the vulnerable point. It is also the most powerful. Such prayer disposes—Ignatius' word—our hearts to receive the love and grace of God there, where we most need it. The Eucharist, Eucharistic Adoration, the Sacrament of Reconciliation, the Liturgy of the Hours, the Scriptures, *lectio divina*, Ignatian meditation and contemplation, the Rosary, and simple prayer from the heart asking God's grace to grow in that area: This is where the effort to strengthen the weak point begins. When we pray in any of these ways, the vulnerable point becomes a space that leads us to God and draws us closer to him.

"Come to me, all you who labor and are burdened, and I will give you rest" (Mt 11:28, NABRE). Bring this place of struggle to the Lord and, with confidence, ask for the help you need.

The Examen

This form of prayer, in a particular way, assists the effort to strengthen the weak point. It is the prayer of daily spiritual awareness. Find help (see the following considerations) toward learning and practicing this blessed prayer.[4]

Spiritual Accompaniment

All that we said regarding rule 13 applies here in a special way. Do not be alone in this effort. Find ways to be

[4] See note 4 in the chapter on rule 6.

accompanied spiritually as you seek this growth. Such accompaniment will help you identify the weak point, allow you to speak about it, provide wise counsel regarding it, show you how to pray about it, and offer encouragement along the way. Accompaniment is key to perseverance in this endeavor, and it cannot be overemphasized.

Spiritual Reading

You are part of a long and rich Catholic spiritual tradition. You are not the first to face this struggle. Learn from the saints and spiritual masters who know it well and provide effective remedies. Read the classic texts and recent Catholic writing of value. Explore pertinent digital resources. Such reading, listening, and viewing will provide new insight and hearten you on the journey.

Nonspiritual Means

If the roots of the spiritually vulnerable point are on the nonspiritual (psychological, physical) level, then appropriate use of nonspiritual means will assist the effort to grow spiritually in that area. Might conversation with a Catholic psychologist or counselor be helpful? When the root of the vulnerability is emotional pain, such conversation may powerfully assist spiritual growth in this area. When physical factors are involved, consulting with doctors and adopting their counsel will likewise assist the effort.

The eagle flies with two wings. When we employ both spiritual and appropriate nonspiritual means in the effort to grow, blessed progress results.

Learning from Venerable Bruno

The life of Venerable Bruno Lanteri exemplifies the gift of rule 14.[5] From a young age, he desired to be "sincere, warm, peaceful, ... joyful, compassionate, accommodating in all that is not offensive to God, gentle, and humble of heart".[6] But it was a long and difficult struggle.

In self-examination, Bruno recognized in himself "severity and roughness with my neighbor".[7] He noted that he was "rough, with little compassion ... impatient, oversensitive in things not to my liking, and therefore sharp in replying to others".[8] Bruno proposed "to make my particular examination on gentleness and humility of heart, and to renew this often, especially in my principal actions".[9]

With great energy and detail, he pursued such gentleness:

> For my particular examination on gentleness, I will read in Rodriguez[10] or elsewhere about the nature, kinds, acts, degrees, aids, obstacles, means and examples of this virtue; from time to time, I will compare my response to others with the way Jesus Christ responds to those he meets; immediately upon arising, I will renew my proposal to grow in this virtue and will ask God's help; I will examine myself often on this virtue and note my failures in writing,

[5] Venerable Bruno Lanteri (1759–1830), founder of the Oblates of the Virgin Mary, my religious community. For resources on him see "Books" at www.discernment.institute, and "Founder" at www.omvusa.org. For a biography of Venerable Bruno, see Timothy Gallagher, O.M.V., *Begin Again: The Life and Spiritual Legacy of Bruno Lanteri* (Crossroad, 2013).

[6] Gallagher, *Begin Again*, 35.

[7] Gallagher, *Begin Again*, 48.

[8] Gallagher, *Begin Again*, 49.

[9] Gallagher, *Begin Again*, 49.

[10] Alonso Rodriguez, S.J. (1526–1616), *The Practice of Christian Perfection*, in three volumes: a classic in multiple editions through the centuries and today, among them Caritas Publishing, 2023.

> even when walking through the streets; before going to bed I will make my particular examination on this and review my progress day by day and week by week.[11]

His pursuit of gentleness was unrelenting. At age sixty-eight, three years before his death, Bruno again wrote, "I will strive to grow in the virtues of humility, gentleness, and confidence."[12]

The fruit of his efforts to strengthen the weak point was evident in his life and ministry. People flocked to his confessional seeking spiritual direction and always left consoled. In the wake of the French Revolution, the director of police in Turin, where Venerable Bruno lived, wrote to his superior in Paris, "He is one of the most sought after [priests] in the city.... Many, among them the most influential persons, have taken him as their spiritual director."[13]

A retreatant described him as "a man who is most gentle"[14] and wrote to his wife, "The superior, Father Lanteri, is very gentle."[15] And again, "For myself, I can tell you that I am very happy with Father Lanteri. I have spent much time with him. I find him gentle, persuasive, and, above all, most considerate. God gives him much light to understand and explain things very well."[16]

Such is the blessed fruit of rule 14: to know the vulnerable point; to seek, with God's grace and without discouragement, growth in that point; and to experience the wonderful liberation that results. Truly, as Saint John of

[11] Gallagher, *Begin Again*, 49–50.
[12] Gallagher, *Begin Again*, 50.
[13] Gallagher, *Begin Again*, 7.
[14] Gallagher, *Begin Again*, 225.
[15] Gallagher, *Begin Again*, 226.
[16] Gallagher, *Begin Again*, 227.

the Cross writes, "Through the practice of one virtue all the virtues grow."[17] Nowhere is this growth more apparent than when, through such efforts and with God's grace, the weak point is transformed.

Witnesses to Rule 14

Saint Thomas Aquinas

The demons know what happens outwardly among men; but the inward disposition of man God alone knows, Who is the *weigher of spirits* (Prov 16:2). It is this disposition that makes man more prone to one vice than to another: hence the devil tempts, in order to explore this inward disposition of man, so that he may tempt him to that vice to which he is most prone.[18]

The counsel of rule 14 is the answer to this tactic of the enemy.

Saint Thérèse of Lisieux

To her sister Marie, discouraged as she compared herself to Thérèse:

Dear Sister, how can you say after this that my desires are the sign of my love? ... Ah! I really feel that it is not this at all that pleases God in my little soul: what pleases Him is *that He sees me loving my littleness* and my *poverty, the blind*

[17] *The Ascent of Mount Carmel*, in *The Collected Works of St. John of the Cross*, 3rd ed., trans. Kieran Kavanaugh, O.C.D., and Otilio Rodriguez, O.C.D. (ICS Publications, 1991), 147.

[18] *Summa Theologica*, trans. Fathers of the English Dominican Province, vol. 1 (Christian Classics, 1981), I, q. 114, a. 2, ad 2, p. 557.

hope that I have in His mercy.... That is my only treasure, dear Godmother, why would this treasure not be yours?[19]

Thérèse's "Copernican Revolution" in the spiritual life: Our weakness, our vulnerability, our littleness, and our poverty are transformed from a source of discouragement to the reason for our greatest confidence. "That is my only treasure.... Why would this treasure not be yours?" Yes, why would it not be yours?

Saint Catherine of Siena

You ask for the will to know and love me, supreme Truth. Here is the way, if you would come to perfect knowledge and enjoyment of me, eternal Life: Never leave the knowledge of yourself. Then, put down as you are in the valley of humility you will know me in yourself, and from this knowledge you will draw all that you need.[20]

Saint John Paul II

In both East and West, we may trace a journey which has led humanity down the centuries to meet and engage truth more and more deeply. It is a journey that has unfolded—as it must—within the horizon of personal self-consciousness: the more human beings know reality and the world, the more they know themselves in their uniqueness, with the question of the meaning of things

[19] *Letters of St. Thérèse of Lisieux*, trans. John Clarke, O.C.D., vol. 2, *1890–1897* (ICS Publications, 1988), 999, italics and ellipses in original. See also, Timothy Gallagher, O.M.V., "The Letters of St. Thérèse", podcast, available on the Discerning Hearts app.

[20] *Catherine of Siena: The Dialogue*, trans. Suzanne Noffke, O.P. (Paulist Press, 1980), 29.

and of their very existence becoming ever more pressing. This is why all that is the object of our knowledge becomes a part of our life. The admonition *Know yourself* was carved on the temple portal at Delphi, as testimony to a basic truth to be adopted as a minimal norm by those who seek to set themselves apart from the rest of creation as "human beings," that is as those who "know themselves."[21]

Self-knowledge renders possible the liberation to which Ignatius calls us in rule 14.

[21] Encyclical letter *Fides at Ratio* (September 14, 1998), no. 1, https://www.vatican.va/content/john-paul-ii/en/encyclicals/documents/hf_jp-ii_enc_14091998_fides-et-ratio.html. For complementary quotations, see Gallagher, *Setting Captives Free*: Venerable Matt Talbot (251–53).

COMMENCEMENT

I cannot call this final word a "conclusion". It is much more a "commencement", in the sense that a graduation ceremony is referred to as a "commencement exercise". The call now is to move from these pages to life: to live the discerning life by exercising Saint Ignatius' fourteen rules in daily life. The fruit of so doing will quickly be evident, and you will bless the resulting new freedom to love and serve God and others.

I warmly recommend that you continue learning about these rules. In the section titled "Additional Resources", I indicate written, audial, and visual ways of doing so. From forty years of sharing these rules, I can promise you that you will love the rewards of such learning.

I find these best expressed in the words with which Jesus summarizes his messianic mission: "He has sent me to proclaim liberty to captives and recovery of sight to the blind, to let the oppressed go free" (Lk 4:18, NABRE). *Setting captives free*—free from discouragement, free from the enemy's lies, free to live our vocations with joy, free to love—is the mission of Jesus. In his fourteen rules, Saint Ignatius is the instrument and servant of that mission.

To begin, or to undertake with new energy the discerning life, I invite you now to pray, without hurry, Pope Leo XIV's lovely prayer for discernment:

> Holy Spirit, you, light of our understanding,
> gentle breath that guides our decisions,

grant me the grace to listen attentively to your
voice
and to discern the hidden paths of my heart,
so that I may grasp what truly matters to you,
and free my heart from its troubles.

I ask you for the grace to learn how to pause,
to become aware of the way I act,
of the feelings that dwell within me,
and of the thoughts that overwhelm me
which, so often, I fail to notice.

I long for my choices
to lead me to the joy of the Gospel.
Even if I must go through moments of doubt and
fatigue,
even if I must struggle, reflect, search, and begin
again ...
Because, at the end of the journey,
your consolation is the fruit of the right decision.

Grant me a deeper understanding of what moves
me,
so that I may reject what draws me away from
Christ,
and love him and serve him more fully.

Amen.[1]

[1] Pope Leo XIV, "Video Message of the Holy Father with the Prayer Intention for the Month of July", July 3, 2025, https://press.vatican.va/content/salastampa/en/bollettino/pubblico/2025/07/03/250703g.html.

ACKNOWLEDGMENTS

I am grateful to all who have helped me in the writing and publishing of this book; to those who read the manuscript and offered comments: James Gallagher, Thomas Gallagher, Dr. Chris and Pat Lynch, Joan Marra, Suzanne O'Neal, and Fr. Mark Yavarone, O.M.V; to Tamara Conley, M.L.I.S., for her invaluable help with library sources; to Dr. David Gallagher for his assistance with quotations from Saint Thomas Aquinas; and to Elizabeth Valeri for her close reading of the text and her skilled editorial assistance. All of these have made this a better book.

To the personnel at Ignatius Press, and, in particular, Thomas Jacobi, Kathy Mosier, Rose Decaen, Nick Frankovich, Sharon Denk, and Sandy Lindemann.

ADDITIONAL RESOURCES

Books by Timothy M. Gallagher, O.M.V.

The Discerning Priest: Ignatian Wisdom for Daily Life in Priesthood (Emmaus Road, 2026).

The Discernment of Spirits: An Ignatian Guide to Everyday Living (Crossroad, 2005).

Discernment of Spirits in Marriage: Ignatian Wisdom for Husbands and Wives (Sophia Institute Press, 2020).

The Examen Prayer: Ignatian Wisdom for Our Lives Today (Crossroad, 2006)

A Reader's Guide to "The Discernment of Spirits: An Ignatian Guide to Everyday Living" (Crossroad, 2013).

Setting Captives Free: Personal Reflections on Ignatian Discernment of Spirits (Crossroad, 2018).

Struggles in the Spiritual Life: Their Nature and Their Remedies (Sophia Institute Press, 2022).

When You Struggle in the Spiritual Life: An Ignatian Path to Freedom (Crossroad, 2021).

Podcasts

"The Discernment of Spirits" on discerninghearts.com, iTunes, Google Play, YouTube, Spotify, Formed, and other platforms. On the Discerning Hearts (free) app: In the opening menu, tap on "Spiritual Formation"; then tap on the image of Father Gallagher. This will lead to the series titled "Discernment of Spirits".

"Ignatian Discernment in Daily Life: Finding God in All Things", on Learn25.com.

Videos

Ten video-recorded talks on the fourteen rules are available at https://ondemand.ewtn.com/Home/Series/catalog/video/en/living-the-discerning-life-the-spiritual-teaching-of-st-ignatius-of-loyola.

Websites

For all of Father Gallagher's materials and for information about the Ignatian Discernment Institute, check out www.discernment.institute.

For information about the Oblates of the Virgin Mary and to explore a vocation to the Oblates, go to www.omvusa.org.